NEW CREATION

Derek Burton

NOTE: The images in this book are free
downloads from the world wide web

This book is dedicated to my wife Marian
with thanks for her patience, support and
advice over many years in the preparation of
the original messages contained within it

CONTENTS

FOREWORD

In *New Creation* Derek continues the work of his earlier book 'A Light To My Path'. Both draw from the same resource – his sermons delivered during his 40 years of Reader ministry.

Again, his themes wander far and wide, through the books of the Bible, the seasons of the Church's year and the joys and challenges facing us all. He examines an extensive range of topics, always seeking to explain just what God means, what he expects of us, and how he facilitates our efforts, and enables us to do his will.

At every juncture, he reminds us what the Scriptures have to say about whatever point he makes.

From the outset Derek makes repeated use of the reality of what the Apostle Paul describes as "spiritual forces of evil", to help us to recognize and oppose such forces, and in so doing contribute to the Great Commission – to make disciples of all people.

It's a book we can dip into here and there, as a particular issue or subject may seize our attention over the months and years.

Tony Garland
Lay Canon Emeritus, Newcastle Cathedral

INTRODUCTION

My book title is derived from the second letter from the Apostle Paul to the church at Corinth chapter 5 verse 17, "Therefore if anyone is in Christ, the new creation has come. The old has gone, the new is here." In Revelation chapter 21 verse 1 we read, "Then I saw a new heaven and a new earth, for the first heaven and the first earth had passed away." And in verse 5, He who was seated on the throne said, "I am making everything new."

I experienced new life in Christ as a student of architecture. When hitch-hiking in Sweden I experienced a severe depression, almost suicidal in intensity. Back in London I picked up some Christian literature from the vestibule of the church of All Souls, Langham Place. In reading this on a train one day, the person of Jesus Christ became vividly real to me, and with the help of the curate at All Souls I made a commitment to my new faith. From that day I was born again, a new creation in Christ

'NEW CREATION' is my second book of studies and is based on a selection of early edited messages preached at my church and other local churches since I was licensed as Reader. As a committed believer in the authority of the Bible as the Word of God, I have tried to preach according to my understanding of the Bible. All the messages have titles which are listed on the Contents index. My prayer is that readers will find the messages helpful in their own spiritual journey, as I have found them in mine.

Derek Burton
Reader Emeritus
Diocese of Newcastle upon Tyne

AUTHOR'S NOTE

Derek Burton is Reader Emeritus in the Church of England Diocese of Newcastle upon Tyne. He is married to Marian, and they have two sons and five grandchildren. Derek qualified as Architect RIBA in 1973, and the family moved from Reigate in Surrey in 1978 when Derek joined Faulkner Browns Architects at Killingworth. He was licensed Reader by the Bishop in Newcastle Cathedral in 1981, and was appointed Emeritus in 2001. After thirteen years at Faulkner Browns, Derek finished his career as Surveyor in the Newcastle Diocese, and retired in 1996. After retirement, he continued in practice as a private architect, with several local projects and culminating in the conversion of a Methodist church into offices for a charity working with homeless young people.

NEW CREATION is based on selected and edited messages preached as sermons over many years. They consist of Biblical exposition and allegory. Each message has a simple theme title and page numbers are clearly listed on the Contents pages.

Messages Titles
in
Alphabetical Order

A Thorn in My Flesh

The Apostle Paul was called by God in the most dramatic way, from the privilege of social status and respect as a Pharisee, to the privilege of suffering for the sake of Jesus Christ and the gospel. But he considered all he had lost as rubbish, compared with the surpassing greatness of knowing Jesus. In his letter to the church at Corinth, he refers to a particular form of suffering which he describes as "a thorn in my flesh, a messenger of Satan to torment me." It was an expression used as a potent symbol of a physical weakness or disability, or an attack on his reputation, perhaps from within the church by jealous false apostles, which would cause the deepest pain. Whatever it was, it was sufficiently painful for Paul to seek release from it by persistent prayer to God, possibly over a long period, until he received a response, which when it came was this: "My grace is sufficient for you, for my strength is made perfect in weakness." Paul was not granted what he asked for, but in gaining understanding and encouragement, was enabled not only to bear his weaknesses, but to boast about them, and even take pleasure in them. This is what he says: "for Christ's sake, I delight in weaknesses, in insults, in hardships, in persecutions, in difficulties. For when I am weak, then I am strong." He had learned an important lesson.

What can we learn from Paul's experience as we ask for wholeness and healing with various problems, weaknesses, disabilities, hardships, difficulties? I am not talking about what we used to call in the army 'self inflicted wounds'; things we bring upon ourselves by our own actions. I am talking about wounds inflicted upon us as part of suffering humanity, and, in particular, attacks by the enemy of souls, because we have chosen to identify ourselves, and to suffer, with Christ.   First, we learn that suffering of all kinds does not come directly from God, but from Satan, whose intention is to torment, discourage and destroy. In the context of the Church, the body of Christ, God, in His sovereign power, sometimes allows this, and can use it for our benefit, and for His glory if we accept it by faith. Because we know that "in all things God works for the good of those who love Him, who have been called according to His purpose." Secondly, it is right for us to bring our distress and pain to God in prayer, and to persist until we receive some response, either directly or indirectly. Our perseverance will indicate our firm resolve in seeking God's will for us. Thirdly, we learn that it is in our weakness that we are made strong, by total dependence upon our God's resources, and not our own.

The message is clear. Satan's purposes are always negative and destructive, because he is a "liar and the father of lies." God the Father's purposes are always positive and constructive because His word is truth and life. The seeming defeat of the cross, and the end of hope, was in fact the greatest victory of all time. Death was swallowed up in victory! The thorns that pierced the head of Jesus were a crown. His pierced body and His blood poured out, gained for us a pardon and the promise of eternal life. So, in spite of 'seemings', in spite of present temporary troubles, let us be encouraged and strengthened in our weakness. For when we are weak, then we are strong.

A Thorn In My Flesh

Angels

There are forces of great power in the world that cannot be seen. Where would we be today without electricity? Can electricity be seen? No, but we can see the effects of it as we switch on a light or plug in to a socket. Who can see the wind, or even know where it comes from? We can only feel the force and see the effects of it. These forces are unseen, powerful and potentially dangerous, but we have learned to use them for our own benefit.

What exists is not only what we can see. There are powerful unseen spiritual forces at work in the world. The title of this message is 'Angels'. What are angels, and what do they do? According to Scripture, angels are spiritual beings who worship God and are His messengers, to serve Him in heaven and help humankind on earth. The heavenly Host refers to angels, and the Scriptures record many occasions when they appear on earth with messages from God, or to strengthen and help people in difficult circumstances. In the hierarchy of angels there are two archangels with special authority, Michael and Gabriel, the only angels that are named. There are also fallen angels whose leader is Satan. If you have been to Coventry Cathedral you will have seen the very powerful sculpture by Sir Jacob Epstein, of the archangel Michael with the devil bound under his feet. This is symbolic of the war in heaven described in Revelation chapter 12, when Michael and his angels fought and defeated a rebellion by Satan (called the dragon) and his angels. Satan is described as the deceiver of the whole world, who accuses us day and night before God. He deceived our first parents from the beginning, causing them to believe a lie, and so bringing us under his power as the prince of this world. He continues to deceive the world, but his power is limited, and he and his angels are doomed to destruction at the final judgment.

Christians are involved in the spiritual battle between good and evil, and cannot remain neutral in it. We must choose whose side we are on. We are those who have made a conscious decision to follow Jesus Christ, and have promised to fight under His banner against sin, the world, and the devil. No one wants to back a loser. We have chosen the Lord of Glory, the Prince of Peace, the Son of the living God. We are on the victory side. Our God works everything for our good, and has given His angels charge of us to guard us in all our ways. The writer of Hebrews tells us that angels are ministering spirits sent to serve those who will inherit salvation. We have every reason to live in hope without fear, being surrounded by angels, just as the prophet Elisha was. The unseen armies of God were all round Elisha, and he couldn't have been more secure, in spite of all appearances to the contrary. So it is with us, but so often we live in fear and trembling, seeing the Church as a fortress to retreat into, instead of one to attack from. This is where we gain our strength and courage, and are built up in the faith, in loving communion with our God, and with each other. Here we see the desperate need of those living without hope, and understand our call to go out into the world to preach the gospel in word and deed, in the power of the Holy Spirit. Angels go before us, and minister to us, just as they have always done with the people of God. An angel ministered to Elijah when he was fleeing from Jezebel. An angel shut the lions' mouths when Daniel was thrown into their den. Angels ministered to our Lord after His temptations by the devil in the desert. An angel rescued Peter from his prison cell, and an angel stood by Paul on the sinking ship, assuring him that all on board would be saved. There are many accounts of angels as messengers. The archangel Gabriel appeared to the Virgin Mary. Angels announced the tidings of great joy to the shepherds. They appeared to Mary Magdalene at the empty tomb, and assured the disciples that their ascended Lord would return in the same way they had seen Him go into heaven. He will indeed come again in glory.

When He does every eye will see Him, and His angels will be with Him. Do we expect to see angels today? Perhaps not, but why not? The writer of Hebrews tells us not to neglect to show hospitality to strangers, for thereby some have entertained angels unawares. We may have had an angel in our home without knowing it.

Let us be encouraged by these thoughts. We are protected on every side even though we may suffer injury and hurt. There are casualties in every war, and we can leave ourselves open to attack, like a sheep when it strays far from the shepherd. The Apostle Paul says that we are not contending against flesh and blood, but against the spiritual forces of wickedness in heavenly places. Our obedience to Christ will bring us into conflict, and spiritual weapons will be required. We shall need the whole armour of God, including the shield of faith and the sword of the Spirit, which is the word of God. What a privilege to be called to be messengers with the good news of eternal salvation through faith in Jesus Christ.   There is no greater news on earth. There will be opposition, difficulty, disappointment, but we cannot fail, because we go in the name of the Lord of Hosts.   The prospect may be daunting, but as Elisha said to his servant, so he says to us: "Fear not, for those who are with us are more than those who are with them." O Lord, open our eyes that we may see around us the horses and chariots of fire that were round about Elisha. These are none other but the angels of our God.

Angels

Aspects of God

"Let us offer to God acceptable worship with reverence and awe; for our God is a consuming fire." *Hebrews 12: 28*

In passages from Exodus and Hebrews we see contrasting aspects of God. The first is visible, tangible, audible, awesome and frightening. The second is silent, peaceful, unseen, merciful, comforting. What are we to make of this? Sometimes, the God we see in the Old Testament, seemingly violent and vengeful, we find difficult to equate with what we see of Him in His Son, Jesus. For this reason, some find it difficult to relate to the Old Testament at all. I believe that if we are to have a mature faith, it is essential for us to come to terms with the whole revelation of Himself that God has given us. We are in the privileged position of being on this side of the Cross, and therefore able to see how God dealt with humankind from the beginning, and how His promise to Abraham has been, and is being, fulfilled. We have more pieces of the puzzle than our fathers had, and so we should be able to go forward with more faith and trust when we see how faithful God has been in His promises. The essential key to the puzzle has been provided, and we have the Holy Spirit to interpret and make real all that God has provided for us in His Son. It is very tempting for us to be content with only a little revelation. We believe enough to give us comfort, but not enough to make us powerful, and weapons in God's hands in the battle against evil. It is tempting to cling to the things we like and avoid the difficulties. Like a child that never grows up, but clings to the comfort blanket and the teddy bear, and won't venture out into the dark. We are not meant to be like that, but to grow to full maturity both physically and spiritually, "That you may stand mature and fully assured in all the will of God." *Colossians 4:12.* Maturity means facing up to reality, not running away from it. Some of the problems Christians have, especially in their relationships with one another, stems from believing that the little bit of truth they understand is all the truth there is, or at least enough of it to satisfy them and base their theology upon.

I believe that it is important for us to come to terms with the aspect of God which is awesome and fearful in order to have a mature understanding of Him. In order to understand the mercy of God, we must first see Him as righteous and perfect Judge in His relentless fight against all that is contrary to His will and purpose. We allow ourselves the passion of righteous indignation in our judgment of those who offend so obviously and grievously against all that is decent and good in our society. Our anger is stirred up and we cry out for justice and vengeance against perpetrators of such heinous crimes. Our attitude and reaction to those in authority, or indeed anyone, depends on four main things. 1. Their position in society. 2. What they look like. 3. What they say. 4. What they do. So it is with our attitude and reaction to God in our perception of who or what He is, and what He says and does. The one who reveals Himself to humankind is none other than the Almighty and Omnipotent God, Creator of all that is, whose laws and commands must be obeyed. We hear what He says in His word, we understand His divine character, and we experience what He does. Our response depends on the depth of our understanding and experience of Him.

The thing that comes over strongly to us in the passage from Hebrews, is holiness. We are to make every effort to live in peace with all people, and to be holy, because without holiness no one will see the Lord. It is a solemn warning and one we should treat seriously. These are the points the writer of Hebrews brings to our attention in connection with holiness: Live in peace with everyone. Avoid bitterness and immorality. Do not treat the things of God lightly or in an off hand manner. Offer to God acceptable worship with reverence and awe. Christians are called to be holy. That is, we are set apart for divine use, consecrated to God. As we look at the holiness of God, we understand it to be the awe-inspiring side of His divine character, His moral excellence. The work of the Holy Spirit is to make us more like Jesus. I think that generally we fear holiness because we do not want to appear to be seen as pious hypocrites, unable to live up to what we profess. The balance we are required to make is to be "In the world, but not of the world." No one pretends it is easy, but we are called to do it, and the means of grace are available to live up to this calling. If we don't, it is because in the end, we don't want to.

As we understand the whole nature of God in His unchanging laws, judgment and mercy, let us seek after holiness.   Let us not emulate the world in our attitudes and conversation, but as the Apostle Paul entreats us: "Be imitators of God as dearly loved children." There must not be even a hint of sexual immorality, impurity or greed, because these are improper for God's holy people. Nor should there be obscenity, foolish talk or coarse joking. We are not to get drunk on wine, but instead be filled with the Spirit. Brothers and sisters in Christ, let us have nothing to do with these fruitless works of darkness, but rather let us seek after God and the holiness without which no one will see the Lord.

Aspects of Prayer

Prayer is the highest activity of which the human spirit is capable. It is communion with God, the Creator of the universe, and is initiated by him. He prompts us to pray as we recognize our need. Prayer is not a 'natural' activity, it is a spiritual activity. No self-sufficient person prays until his self-sufficiency proves false, i.e. in times of trouble and danger.

Types of prayer:-
Adoration: Expressing our love for, and worship of, our divine Creator God.
Matthew 22: 3 7- "You shall love the Lord your God with all your heart, and with all your soul, and with all your mind."
Confession: Acknowledging that we are sinners and deserving of judgment.
1 John 1: 19 - "If we confess our sins, He is faithful and just to forgive us our sins and to cleanse us from all unrighteousness."
Repentance: Expressing our sorrow for our sins and resolving to turn away from all forms of evil. *Matthew 3: 8 Produce fruit in keeping with repentance."*
Intercession: the act of offering petitionary prayer on behalf of others. *James 5:16 - "Therefore confess your sins to one another, and pray for one another, so that you may be healed."*
Supplication: turning to God to receive something, making known our desires. *Philippians 4: 6 - "Do not worry about anything, but in everything by prayer and supplication with thanksgiving let your requests be made known to God".*
Thanksgiving: giving thanks for all things unto God the Father in the name of our Lord Jesus Christ. *Psalm 92:1 - "It*

is good to give thanks to the Lord, to give thanks to your name, O Most High".

<u>Praise:</u> praise and thanksgiving are closely akin to each other. *Psalm 146:7 - "I will praise the Lord as long as I live: I will sing praises to my God all my life long"*.

<u>Conversation:</u> the free and natural exchange of ideas between people. Share everything with God; joys, sorrows, worries etc. Good conversations involve both talking and listening. *John 10:27- "My sheep hear my voice. I know them and they follow me"*.

<u>Prayer without words:</u> God knows when we can't put it into words. Just be in his presence in silence. *Romans 8: 26 - "Likewise the Spirit helps us in our weakness; for we do not know how to pray as we ought, but that same Spirit intercedes with sighs too deep for words"*.

<u>Prayer is an offensive weapon</u>, part of the Christian's armoury. *Ephesians 6:1 - "Therefore take up the whole armour of God, so that you may be able to stand on that evil day, and having done everything, to stand firm"*. Together with the Sword of the Spirit, which is the word of God, we attack enemy strongholds and enlarge God's kingdom. Prayer is not an easy way of getting what we want, but a difficult way of becoming what God wants us to be. Jesus gave us prayer for our benefit. It is the means by which we connect ourselves with Him.

Problems when we pray: Answers to prayer is not dependent upon our emotions or our thoughts before, during or after prayer. Faith does not depend on how we feel. We vacillate between doubt and faith, not certain whether we are praying aright, according to God's will or not. There seems little earnestness and sincerity, and we doubt we will be heard. We must tell him about our doubts and weak faith. We have given him access and he will fulfil our hearts' desires. To pray is difficult for all of us. Don't expect it to be easy. It can feel like too much of an effort. It becomes a burden if we think our Lord is strict and insists it should be done. There should be no guilt for failure. We need practice and perseverance, and need to be motivated. It is for our benefit. It is a powerful weapon against evil. There are wonderful promises concerning prayer in the Scriptures.

Common Mistakes
<u>We think we must help God to fulfil our prayer.</u> To pray is to tell Jesus what we lack. Intercession is to tell Jesus what others lack. At the wedding at Cana the mother of Jesus did not suggest what he should do; she just told him, "they have no wine". She left it with him knowing he would do something. Our prayer life will become restful when it really dawns on us we have done all we are supposed to do when we have spoken to him about it. <u>We forget to pray in the name of Jesus.</u> It is our Lord Jesus who intercedes for us at the right hand of God the Father. *Romans 8 :34 - "It is Christ Jesus, who died, yes, who was raised, who is at the right hand of God, who indeed intercedes for us". John 14:13 -   "I will do whatever you ask in my name, so that the Father may be glorified in the Son".* <u>We pray with wrong motives.</u> How can I in the best way, make use of God for my own personal advantage? We tend to pray selfishly for the things which concern us personally, (our preaching, our meeting, etc.) *James 4:3 - "You ask and do not receive, because you ask wrongly, in order to spend what you get on your pleasures".* <u>Do not be put off by the difficulties.</u> Remember practice and perseverance; tests of our true desires. What do we really

want? Is it our deepest desire to draw near to God, for a closer walk with him? Perhaps we are afraid of what he may ask of us. Remember he loves you, and has only your greatest good at heart. <u>Drawing near to God.</u> It is true that we can pray anywhere, at any time, but is that ideal? It's a matter of priorities. We really need to set aside specific times for prayer, perhaps early in the morning? It is helpful to combine reading the Bible and prayer. What we read can trigger off, praise, confession, intercession, etc. There are various helps and methods for reading the Bible, for example, 'Daily Notes' or 'Daily Bread', or the 'Bible Reading Fellowship' daily readings and notes. <u>Encouragements for Prayer.</u> *Luke 11:9,10 - "So I say to you, ask and it will be given to you, search and you will find, knock and the door will be opened for you. For everyone who asks receives, and everyone who searches finds, and for everyone who knocks, the door will be opened".* The prayer of humankind is one of the most effective means by which God directs the world forward towards its goal, the kingdom of God.

Christian Mission

According to Wikipedia, Christian Mission is defined as, "an organized effort to spread Christianity. This involves evangelism, preaching a set of beliefs for the purpose of conversion, and humanitarian work, especially among the poor and disadvantaged. Missionaries have the authority to preach the Christian faith, and provide humanitarian work to improve economic development, literacy, education, health care and orphanages."

The earliest examples of Christian missionary activity are those recorded in writings that would eventually come to form the New Testament. Early writings include the letters of the Apostle Paul who, as the Pharisee, Saul of Tarsus, was an active persecutor of Christians, until his own conversion on the road to Damascus, as recorded in the Acts of the Apostles. Saul's conversion was the result of an encounter with the risen Christ, when he heard the words, "Saul, Saul, why are you persecuting me?" The commission of Jesus Christ to Saul was - "I am sending you to the Gentiles, to open their eyes so that they may turn from darkness to light and from the power of Satan to God, so that they may receive forgiveness of sins and a place among those who are sanctified by faith in me." *Acts 26: 17,18.* Saul, as the Apostle Paul, became the greatest evangelist the world has ever known. His letters to the churches are accepted as canons of Scripture.

After the birth of the Church at Pentecost, the Spirit filled preaching of the Apostle Peter and the acts of all the Apostles, the commission of Jesus to Saul, must surely be vitally important in our understanding of the essential nature of mission of the Church today. Of course, it all depends on whether we believe that it is the inspired word of God or not. If we do, then it becomes a mainspring of mission. It highlights the following propositions - The Apostle Paul is a chosen instrument of Jesus Christ for the proclamation of the gospel of salvation. There is such a person as Satan, the devil, who tempted Jesus in the desert, is identified by Jesus as a liar and the father of lies, and the god of this world, and who keeps people as slaves to sin and all kinds of evil. We need to be delivered from that slavery which is to turn from darkness to light. Jesus Himself is our Deliverer as we turn to Him in faith for forgiveness of sins, and so become free and purified from corruption, and receive assurance of the gift of eternal life. Is this the essence of the gospel message which the Church is called to proclaim?

Surely, this is far more than humanitarian work among the poor and disadvantaged? It is about calling lost souls from darkness to light, from hell to the kingdom of God. What other world religion can do this? As Jesus Himself says, "I am the Way, the Truth, and the Life. No one can come to the Father except through me." *John 14: 6.* The Apostle Peter, filled with the Holy Spirit says, "There is salvation in no one else, for there is no other name under heaven, given to humankind by which we must be saved." *Acts 4: 12.* Do we believe in the Divine inspiration of Scripture? The established Church of England does, which is why its liturgy confidently proclaims after every reading of Scripture, "This is the Word of the Lord", and, "This is the Gospel of Christ". It is the basis of Christian statement of faith in the Nicene Creed and the Apostle's Creed, all firmly based on Scripture. As individual professing Christians, we are free to believe this or not, but corporately we proclaim it every time we meet together for worship. This is the faith of the Church. Study and interpretation is one thing. Doubt ridden questioning is something else.

What are we trying to do in Mission? What is our motivation for doing it? Jesus calls us to go and make disciples, but we are free to ask the question, "Why"?   What are we hoping to achieve?   Why don't we just leave people alone to get on with their lives as best they can, except where there is obvious humanitarian suffering which we can do something about? Is that it? How can we come to a consensus as a church of committed Christians? What have we got that we must share with those who do not have it? According to Scripture - "Every one of us must appear before the judgment seat of Christ to receive what has been done in the body whether good or bad"- *2 Corinthians 5:10.* Do we believe in the final separation of sheep and goats as in the parable of Jesus in Matthew 25: 31 – 46? Will God say to some, "Depart from me, I never knew you"? Or do we believe in God's love but not His justice?

As Christians, we proudly call ourselves saints, which is what Scripture says we are, as forgiven sinners. In one way or another, either suddenly or over a period of time, we have had an encounter with Jesus Christ, and have responded to His call just as Saul of Tarsus did. Is the commission of Jesus to us, the same in essence as it was to Saul?   Scripture makes it clear that it is a spiritual battle in which the Church of Jesus Christ is engaged. Whatever our particular theological persuasion, we are assured that the battle is not ours, but God's. We are called to take part by faith, as obedient soldiers, and to follow where God leads, but this surely requires total commitment and persistent prayer.

The early eighteenth century philosophy movement, known as the 'Age of Enlightenment', or the 'Age of Reason', has had a considerable influence on Christian theology. The Enlightenment included a range of ideas centred on reason as the primary source of authority, and to advance ideals like liberty, progress, tolerance, and separation of Church and State. It was marked by an emphasis on the scientific method and increased questioning of religious orthodoxy. This gave rise to liberal interpretations of the Bible as being not a collection of factual statements, but allegorical, emphasizing the moral or other spiritual lessons which can be learned from its stories. Liberal Christians placed less emphasis on miraculous events associated with the life of Jesus than on his teachings. Many liberals prefer to read Jesus' miracles as metaphorical narratives for understanding the power of God. Liberal Christian theologians often reject traditional Christian teaching on subjects such as the Virgin Birth, the Resurrection, and the authority of Scripture.

One of the greatest evangelists in eighteenth century England, with John Wesley, was George Whitefield (pronounced Whitfield), a Church of England clergyman. His spiritual devotion was established upon his immovable commitment to the Bible. The more he immersed himself in the Bible, the deeper he grew in his dedication to know God and to advance His kingdom. He devoted himself to the study of the Scriptures and it became like a fire upon the altar of his soul, fuelling his love for Christ. Whitefield was being prepared to be loosed upon the world with the good news of Jesus Christ. He grieved over the eclipse of Scripture in his generation, boldly asserting, "If we once get above our Bibles and cease making the written Word of God our sole rule both as to faith and practice, we shall soon lie open to all manner of delusion and be in great danger of making shipwreck of faith and a good conscience." The Word of God became the ruling authority over his life. It marked the trail upon which he constantly discovered beautiful vistas of redemption, sacrifice, love, and joy. He desired to become more like his Lord with every word he read. Thousands were brought to faith in Christ by Whitefield's preaching.

Christ the Healer

A builder missed his footing on a ladder and fell eight feet from a roof, receiving multiple injuries. There is a law of gravity which must be treated with respect and care if we are not to be harmed by it. This law always applies on earth, unless another law cancels it out, or reduces its effects. No one in their right mind would jump out of an aeroplane without a parachute, or put their hand into a blazing fire. We cannot defy the laws of nature without being hurt or even killed, but we are able to harness and co-operate with them for our wellbeing and benefit. The physical laws involved in the design and deployment of a parachute reduce the speed of a body falling from a great height, and bring it to land without harm. We do this in many ways to protect ourselves from forces that otherwise might cause injury. The forces such as fire, wind and water which we need to sustain life, when out of control, or not treated with care, can do us harm. We do not understand so called natural disasters such as earthquakes and volcanic eruptions which result in such devastation and death. Is God in control, we ask, and why does He allow such things? We have no answer to these questions, except that in some way the whole of creation has been affected by humanity's rebellion against the authority of God. The Apostle Paul describes the whole of creation being in bondage to decay, and that it groans as in the pains of childbirth, awaiting deliverance and renewal. We have an inherited disposition to disobey God's moral laws. This is the true nature of our condition, and it is only when we acknowledge it as fact, that we can begin to seek a remedy. "If we say we have no sin we deceive ourselves and the truth is not in us." It is sin that is at the root of all disease. But just as we have a disposition to sin, fortunately for us the body has a disposition for healing. For example, when we cut a finger, unless we have some genetic defect, the blood clots and allows the wound to close and heal. There is resistance within to fight infection which invades the body, a battle between healthy and infected blood cells. Medicine comes in to help the natural healing process to reinforce resistance to the invading enemy. It is the force of life which fights for survival against the odds. Plants seek to be fruitful and multiply and overcome disasters such as fire. A devastated forest suddenly springs to life again out of the ashes from seeds which have lain dormant for years, awaiting the right conditions of light and heat to suit their germination. Some seeds only pop out of their pods when subjected to intense heat. There is conflict in all this, a struggle between opposing forces of life and death, but always hope of renewal. All that we see in the world throughout history must be seen in the context of the reality of humanity's rebellion against their Creator, the seriousness of sin and its consequences. Defying moral laws has inevitable effects, just as defying natural laws does. Freedom means the right to choose, and if there is only one choice there can be no freedom.

Giuseppe the carpenter, who created the puppet Pinocchio, wanted a real live son to love, and one who would love him. Not one without a heart he could control and manipulate. But when the miracle happened, the boy was free to choose, and was faced with, and succumbed to, harmful influences. Our love and obedience to our heavenly Father, has to come from the heart, freely given and not by coercion. Could we be satisfied with anything less from our children? The wrong choice made by our first parents resulted in their banishment from the presence of God, and from the perfect environment in which He had placed them. They had transferred their allegiance to a false god, and forfeited their inheritance, and so have all their children down through the ages. But in the love and foreknowledge of God, He had a plan for healing and restoration. "God was in Christ reconciling the world to Himself", *2 Corinthians 5:19*. Our Lord Jesus came to heal and restore in the fullest possible way. Physical healing is only a part of what it means to be made whole. He came to heal and restore the whole person, body, soul, and spirit. In the account of the ten lepers who were healed, in the Gospel of Luke, only one came back to give praise and thanks to God. To this one alone, Jesus was able to say, "Rise and go, your faith has made you well." When people suffer in some way, whether physically or mentally, or some personal misfortune, we often hear them say, "What have I done to deserve this?" There seems to be a common assumption that what we are going through is a direct result of something we have done. This may sometimes in fact be correct, for example with drugs, alcohol and sex abuse. We try to reason it out, but in the end we have to acknowledge that God is sovereign, and that He does what He wills to bring about His purposes. There is a law of sin and death, but in the mercy of God there is another law superior to it. If I drop an object to the ground, the law of gravity applies. But if I place my hand underneath to catch it, a superior law cancels out the other law. In His sacrifice on the cross, our Lord Jesus has cancelled the effects of sin. As the Apostle Paul puts it, "The law of the Spirit of life in Christ Jesus, has set me free from the law of sin and death." One day He will come again in glory, and the whole creation will rejoice. The prophet Isaiah puts it beautifully like this, "You will go out with joy, and be led forth in peace; the mountains and the hills will burst forth before you, and all the trees of the field will clap their hands."   *Isaiah 5:12*

Citizens of Heaven

Today we are in heaven! Well, if not actually in heaven, we can be assured that we are 'Citizens of Heaven'. It sounds good, but what does it mean? What is a citizen, and what or where is heaven? A citizen is someone who has rights, duties and protection relating to a town or city. We are citizens of where we live, where our homes are, where we belong. We have rights to supplies of water, electricity and gas; rights to education for our children. We have duties to pay rates and taxes, and obey the law. We have the protection of the legal system and local government regulations. To some people the idea of heaven is "pie in the sky when you die", an illusory hope of something good in the future. To the Christian, heaven has more substance than that, but it cannot be described in terms of a geographical location, but rather a new dimension, beyond time, eternal. It is where the throne of God is. It is where Jesus came from, and what makes it real and exciting for us, it is where He is now, and where He promises we shall be too. We say "our Father in heaven". Jesus says to His followers: "In my Father's house there are many rooms; if it were not so, I would have told you. I go to prepare a place for you, so that where I am you may be also." This is the inheritance of all who believe and trust in Jesus Christ. Not "pie in the sky when you die", but what the Apostle Paul describes as – "A living hope, through the resurrection of Jesus Christ from the dead, to an inheritance incorruptible and undefiled, and that does not fade away, reserved in heaven for you, who are kept by the power of God through faith for salvation ready to be revealed in the last time." - *1 Peter 1:3.* Inheritance speaks of possessions passed down from generation to generation. You don't earn or buy them; you receive them simply because you are a family member because someone has died. Through faith we are one with Christ in His death and resurrection, and because He has been made the heir of everything. As believers, we share the divine son-ship by adoption. We too are made heirs according to promise. We have no need to fear the loss of our inheritance because it is under God's own watchful care, "reserved in heaven for you". It is an inheritance incorruptible and undefiled, and that does not fade away. Unlike any inheritance we may receive here on earth which is corruptible and defiled and which does fade away. Here, the god of this world holds sway, and although the kingdom of God is established, the Father's will is either completely ignored or only imperfectly done.

We say "Thy kingdom come. Thy will be done on earth as it is in heaven." That is our prayer; that is our desire as we see the results of humankind's rebellion against the will and authority of our Creator. The Scripture says that in the end times people's hearts will fail them because of fear, because of what they see coming on the world   *Luke 21:26.* Most people, especially those with young children, will be fearful for their future as they see in our culture the results of permissiveness, unrestrained freedom of expression. I think that the late Margaret Thatcher was right when she wrote this article in the Daily Telegraph: "The younger generation is being reared in a morally corrosive atmosphere where they are taught that in the name of freedom anything goes." This is spiritual anarchy. As the prophet Hosea said – "They sow the wind, and they shall reap the whirlwind." Heaven is where God's will is done perfectly and absolutely, and where there is perfect peace and harmony and joy. No wonder we pray as our Lord taught us: "Thy will be done on earth as it is in heaven." We don't know what heaven will be like. It is not beyond our imagination, but beyond our understanding, because we are locked into our earthly time controlled existence. As a small boy I used to look up at the sky and the stars and wonder what was beyond them. There seems to no limit to space.   The Revelation to John describes heaven in symbolic language, but this passage from chapter 21 is quite clear- "The dwelling of God is with men, and He will live with them and be their God. He will wipe away every tear from their eyes. There will be no more death or mourning or crying or pain, for the old order of things has passed away." He who is seated on the throne said: "I am making everything new." Remember your inheritance.   The Apostle Peter says we are aliens in this world, but we are citizens of heaven and recipients of immeasurable blessings in Christ. In Christ, heaven is our home where we belong, and where we shall live forever with rights, duties and protection as citizens. We must not be too heavenly minded as to be no earthly use. We have much work to do in God's purpose to extend His kingdom here on earth. In Proverbs 14 verse 34 we read this: "Righteousness exalts a nation." This is where eternal choices are made. Without Christ and His Church, political parties won't bring about national repentance and spiritual revival, in spite of their promises and good intentions.

Citizens of heaven have made their choice: they have cast their vote, and Jesus Christ is the only way, for no one comes to the Father except through Him. Our children's future depends on what we teach them, through what we do and say, and what we are. So let us work and pray that our children, and those who who do not yet know Jesus Christ, will themselves become citizens of heaven; to receive an inheritance incorruptible and undefiled, and that does not fade away, reserved in heaven for them.

Communication

To communicate is to make known, reveal, make understandable, share, be in contact, on the same wavelength. What we call the 'media', newspapers, TV, internet, is the way we communicate, locally, nationally and globally. It seems that for most people, if there is a Creator of the universe, whoever it is remains unseen, remote and uncaring about what goes on in the world. But Christians believe that there is a Creator we call God, who does care, who loves, and who communicates with those who search for Him. We say 'Him', because He has chosen to reveal Himself as 'Father' in heaven. We are created beings, not puppets, but with minds and hearts to respond to our Creator, and to have a loving personal relationship with Him

How has this God chosen to communicate with the people He has created to enjoy His company? With all the senses we have been given, we can appreciate the wonder of the created universe, and especially the earth on which we live and breathe and have our being. We have the freedom to interpret this as scientifically explained, initiated by the Big Bang, and progressing through evolution. Or we can believe in God who created everything in the beginning, and who sustains it by His will and power. This is not to deny scientific evidence, but to see in it the hand of a designer Creator. Christians believe that God created humankind in His own image, that is to say, with creative ability and with minds to explore and understand the nature of the universe and its Creator. But our first parents lost their loving, trusting relationship with God by believing a lie, and became subject to a usurper, 'the god of this world', Satan, and became enslaved by him.

We do not need the Bible to remind us that this is a fallen world. The media communicates the fact on a daily basis. What can the Church of Jesus Christ do in such a world? We have a gospel to communicate, the message of salvation through faith and trust in Jesus Christ. This is the gospel message conveyed by the Apostles to a fallen world, and one which the Church of Jesus Christ has been commanded to make known throughout the world. Christ came as a light into the world, and was, in His divine nature, essentially one with the Father, and so, "God was in Christ, reconciling the world to Himself." There is no more powerful a message to be found anywhere else.

In the Gospel of John chapter 5, we see the importance of Scripture with reference to the life and work of Jesus. After all, apart from the Bible, we would know virtually nothing about Him. It is in Scripture that God communicates His very nature as holy, perfectly just in all His ways, and loving towards humankind. Christians need to be diligent in studying the word of God, to grow in knowledge and understanding, and establish a close relationship with Him and His Son, Jesus Christ. The statement of our belief as Christians, the Nicene Creed, is firmly based on Scriptural truth. If we are to communicate, share, make known, God's truth to people in thrall to the 'father of lies', we must be secure in our faith in Jesus, who is the Way, the Truth and the Life.

Compromise

Compromise is defined as 'settlement of a dispute by concessions on both or all sides'. The sense in which the Apostle John uses it is human society organising itself without God, following its own wisdom, and living by the light of its own reason. Let's look at how this operates in everyday life today, in the life of our Lord Jesus, and in the Church in its relation to the world. Common expressions for compromise are, come to terms, meet half way, middle ground, give and take, etc. Life would be very difficult, if not impossible, without compromise, if no one was prepared to make concessions of any kind. Just imagine life at home or at work, without any 'give and take'. But there does come a point where compromise has to stop. Some points of principle or conviction must be fought for, and even, in extreme cases, died for. The opposite extreme of 'peace at any price' can be very costly. In the 1930's, Great Britain's Prime Minister, Neville Chamberlain, obtained a worthless piece of paper signed by Adolf Hitler, and proclaimed, 'Peace in our Time'. Who can measure the price of that peace? The eventual conflict was costly enough in terms of human life, but who can doubt that such evil had to be resisted to the death?

As we look at the life and work of our Lord Jesus Christ, we see that His purpose in coming into the world was to save sinners, but He met with such violent opposition. Human society, organising itself without God, following its own wisdom and living by the light of its own reason, would not acknowledge the divine authority of Christ. In effect saying, "We will not have this man to rule over us." Behind this human rebellion lay the unseen forces of evil, the spiritual hosts of wickedness in the heavenly places, whose leader had perpetrated the deception which brought humankind into the bondage of lies. Jesus did not come to compromise with such forces, but to confront them head on and defeat them, and in so doing, to release those who were enslaved by them. He came to claim back what is rightly God's, to establish the kingdom of God on earth. As people recognised the truth of their condition before God, and the extent of His love for them, they would turn away from lies, and give their allegiance to the one who is the Truth. There could be no give and take, no middle ground between the truth of God and the lies of the devil. From its secure position in Christ, the Church is called to minister to the world in its lost condition, in fact to be Jesus Christ to the world. We need to reconcile two seemingly contradictory ideas in the Scriptures concerning friendship with the world. The Apostle James says, "Whoever wishes to be a friend with the world makes himself an enemy of God", but our Lord Jesus was called, "The friend of tax-collectors and sinners." He scandalised the religious leaders of His day by the company He associated with; down and outs, lepers, prostitutes, adulterers, demon-possessed. His closest friends were a motley collection of uneducated fishermen, and even a hated tax-collector. But He said, "I came not to call the righteous, but sinners to repentance." He saw people as sheep without a shepherd, and had compassion on them in their poverty and sickness, teaching and healing them, bringing life in all its fullness to those who were helpless and hopeless. A friend of the world in the sense which James uses it, is one who habitually enjoys its company, and adopts its standards of behaviour.

It is necessary for us to fully understand the essential difference between the Church and the world. The Church consists of those who have been delivered from human society organising itself without God, and have been placed into Christ. That is what I believe salvation means. We have passed from death to life, a new dimension which does not cease with this earthly existence, but is eternal. This life is open to all who will turn to Christ. We are called in His name to go into the world, and proclaim release to the captives, recovering of sight to the blind, to set at liberty those who are oppressed. It is a high calling, and in our own strength we are inadequate for the task. But we go out with all the authority and power of our Lord Jesus Christ at our disposal.

Let us then, recognise our true potential, the nature of our calling as lights in the world, the salt of the earth, a preserving agent. The world, looks to the Church for truth, the reality behind the words, and is often disappointed. Instead it sees internal political squabbles and sordid scandals, Christians trapped by compromise with evil, and not living according to the truth as it has been revealed in Christ. We are to be in the world, but not of the world. Let us be determined, by God's grace, not to compromise with the world. The Apostle Peter sums it up like this - "But you are a chosen race, a royal priesthood, a holy nation, God's own people, that you may declare the wonderful deeds of Him who called out of darkness into His marvellous light."

Confidence in Christ

"There is no salvation in anyone else at all, for there is no other name under heaven granted to men by which we must be saved." - *Acts 4:12.* That's clear enough isn't it? There is no other way of salvation than through Jesus Christ. To check out this statement we need to refer back to the Gospels to see whether our Lord Jesus made such a positive claim about Himself. We see in fact that He did, and that the Apostle Peter is fully justified in saying what he did. This is what Jesus said. "I am the Way, the Truth, and the Life, no one comes to the Father except through me." He also said - "All authority is given to me in heaven and on earth", and, "If you have seen me, you have seen the Father." There can be no doubt about the incredible claims He made about Himself, and it is our Christian faith that we believe Him. Yet we find it difficult to say that all other religions of the world are delusions, and have no truth in them. We may grant that God has given them some light in a way they can respond to, but there will be only one Perfect Judge on that day when the secrets of all hearts will be revealed. One of the last things Jesus said to His followers was - "Go and make disciples of all nations, baptizing them in the name of the Father, and of the Son, and of the Holy Spirit." This is a command not a request, and one which must be obeyed. It is one that Christian missionaries have lived and died for over centuries.

Some Christians cannot positively say they are sure of their place in heaven, and when challenged can only say, "I hope so". It could be because to some extent they think it depends on them. Look at the well known verse in the Bible, *John 3:16* - "God loved the world so much that He gave His only begotten Son, that whoever believes in Him should not perish, but have everlasting life." There is no lack of assurance here.

All believers are one with Christ, and whatever is true of Him is true of us. He died, we died with Him. He rose from the dead; we shall rise with Him. He ascended into heaven; He has made us sit with Him in the heavenly places. The Scriptures tell us of the riches that are ours in Christ. If only we know it, we are wealthy beyond belief. Our treasure is in heaven, and one day we shall obtain the fullness of it. We should not live as spiritual paupers here. We are a royal Priesthood, sons and daughters of the King of all creation. This is the confidence we are meant to have. Not presumption, but assurance that comes with believing what God has said and done. It sometimes does us good to remind God of His promises to us. Not of course, that He needs reminding about anything, but it strengthens our faith to repeat them back to Him. Some products undergo stringent tests to see if they are fit for what they were intended. Some are tested to the very limit, but not destroyed.

I cannot forget my first encounter with Jesus Christ. A specific moment in time when Jesus became a living reality and not just a remote figure of history. Others may have come to faith very gradually, hardly knowing it had happened, and even not remembering a time when they did not have faith. God deals with us so very differently because He knows us so intimately as individuals. My close encounter came after a time of great spiritual desolation, almost suicidal in intensity. Then in due time came the revelation, an oasis in the desert, a spiritual vision to heal a sick soul, something to be desired more than any treasure. The beauty and love of Jesus who says, "I will never leave you nor forsake you."

If we are lacking assurance, then let us listen to the words of Jesus with a believing heart, "Most assuredly I say to you, he who hears my word and believes in Him who sent me has everlasting life, and shall not come into judgment, but has passed from death to life."

Conflict

The preacher's task is to communicate in the clearest possible way, having earnestly sought in prayer to be an instrument through which God will speak to His people. The responsibility of the hearers is to discern what God is saying to them through His servant, and by His Spirit reject what is false or unhelpful. What is relevant to one may be of no particular value to another. God is able to direct and guide a whole church and specific individuals, through one message.

Our Lord Jesus said some very controversial things we find hard to understand. Coming from the lips of the Prince of Peace, we may find this as recorded by Luke somewhat confusing, "Do you think I came to bring peace on earth? No, I tell you, not at all, but division." - *Luke 12: 51.* Even members of families would be divided against each other. Why? Surely He came to promote love and understanding between people didn't He? Our lives are full of questions, trying to make sense of the world we live in, and in relation to what we read in the word of God. We find conflict everywhere in the world today, and indeed throughout history; international, national, local, community, family, and even within ourselves. Jesus came to heal the division that exists between us and our Creator because of sin, and in so doing had to confront the forces of evil, and the personification of evil who had brought humanity into bondage, the devil. Conflict is a struggle between opposing forces, and all the conflicts in the world resolve themselves into two opposing forces, those that are for God, and those that are against Him. Good and evil, love and hate, truth and lies, light and darkness; that is the essence of it.

Into this conflict came our Lord Jesus Christ as the personification of goodness, love, truth and light, to expose the nature of evil and destroy it. He first had to come in the weakness of the flesh, in humility and apparent defeat, to provide the perfect way for humankind to be forgiven, before He would come again in glory, to judge and beat down Satan forever.   No wonder there was conflict, and there will be conflict until the end of time. What relevance has this for us today? First of all, it means that we should not be surprised when difficulties and conflicts arise around and within us. If we think that because we are Christians everything should be a bed of roses, then we are sadly mistaken. In some ways things could be a whole lot worse if we are called upon to suffer for the sake of the gospel. 'No gains without pains' is a common saying. There is conflict as we seek to know the Lord's will for us. He takes no pleasure in those who put their hand to the plough and look back. Forward is the only way. Standing still is going backwards. The life of faith is not for the fainthearted. The promised land became a reality as God's people entered into it. The impossible became possible when the walls of Jericho fell, because the people were obedient to the call to go forward.

In the Gospels we see the opposition our Lord had to face, mostly from where you would not expect to find it, the religious leaders of the day, the Pharisees. They were always trying to catch Him out with awkward questions, but He knew what was in their minds and hearts, and reduced them to silence by His answers. They accused Him of driving out demons by the prince of demons. This was plainly nonsense as Jesus clearly demonstrated, but they were so twisted in their logic. If they had acknowledged what He was doing was from God, then they would have to acknowledge Him as the Messiah, or at least a prophet. There is conflict in the Church today and division over various issues such as the role of women, and homosexuality. We need to be careful with our conclusions, or we might find ourselves in the position of the Pharisees, calling good evil, and white black. Study of the word of God, and a life of prayer on a consistent daily basis are the means by which we discern the work of the Holy Spirit, and become mature to make spiritual judgments on such issues. Having searched the Scriptures, and his own heart and conscience, Martin Luther came to the point where he could say concerning his faith, "Here I stand, I can do no other." We must do the same in all the conflicts which surround us, in things which affect our ministry and witness here.

If we concentrate our minds too much on division and conflict, we may well become disheartened. It is by faith that we look beyond the present difficulties, beyond the wilderness to the promised land. The Apostle Paul helps us when he says, "This light momentary affliction is preparing for us an eternal weight of glory beyond all comparison" -   2 *Corinthians 4:17,18.*   We obtain encouragement from the prophet Isaiah when he says - "Strengthen the feeble hands, steady the knees that give way; say to those with fearful hearts, 'Be strong, do not fear' your God will come, He will come with vengeance; with divine retribution He will come to save you." - *Isaiah 35:3.*

Crucifixion

Isaiah 52: 13 – 15 and Isaiah 53

We see in these passages from the Prophet Isaiah, the amazingly accurate prophecy of the crucifixion of our Lord Jesus Christ. It reads almost like a first hand factual account, and this, some 700 years or so before the actual event! Marcus Tullius Cicero, the Roman statesman, politician and scholar, described crucifixion as "the most cruel and hideous, of tortures." After sentencing had been passed, it was the custom for the victim to be scourged with the flagellum, a whip of leather thongs with small pieces of metal or bone tied to them. Eusebius, the third century church historian, described Roman flogging like this - the sufferer's veins were laid bare, and the very muscles, sinews and bowels of the victim were open to exposure. After this treatment, our Lord Jesus was taken to the Praetorium, where a crown of thorns was thrust upon His head. He was mocked by a battalion of 600 men, and hit about the face and head. He was then forced to carry a heavy cross bar on His bleeding shoulders until He collapsed, and Simon of Cyrene was press-ganged into carrying it for Him. This is described in Isaiah 52:14 - "his appearance was so disfigured beyond that of of any man, and His form beyond any human likeness."

When they reached the site of crucifixion, Jesus was stripped naked. He was laid on the cross, and six inch nails were driven into His forearms, just above the wrist. His knees were twisted sideways so that the ankles could be nailed between the tibia and Achilles tendon. He was lifted upon the cross which was then dropped into a socket in the ground. There He was left to hang in unthinkable pain, in intense heat and unbearable thirst, exposed to the ridicule of the crowd. Death by this method was usually quite protracted, rarely supervening before 36 hours. The pain was intense, as the whole body was strained, while the hands and feet, which are a mass of nerves and tendons, would lose little blood., causing a throbbing headache, and eventually traumatic fever would set in. When for any reason it was proposed to put the sufferer out of his misery before the end, the legs were shattered with blows from a club or hammer.

It was in the Scriptures that our Lord Jesus recognised His mission and purpose as He grew to manhood, and it must have been in the graphic passages from Isaiah that He would have seen the manner of death He was to die. Yet, knowing all that in advance, He turned His face towards Jerusalem in obedience to His Father's will. The Suffering Servant. Yet the worst part of His suffering was not only the physical trauma and torture of crucifixion, and the emotional pain of being rejected by the world, and deserted by His friends, but the spiritual agony of being cut off from His Father for us as He carried our sins. The words of the well, known hymn say - "We may not know, we cannot tell, what pains He had to bear, but we believe it was for us He hung and suffered there." In the separation between Father and Son, it seems the very Godhead was torn apart! But it was for this that our Lord Jesus came, not only to die for our sins, but to rise again in triumph from the grave, that we might live! And this is the gospel, the good news that we are to proclaim to those who are dead in trespasses and sins, so that they can see the extent of the love of God in Christ, and respond in repentance and faith, out of darkness into light.

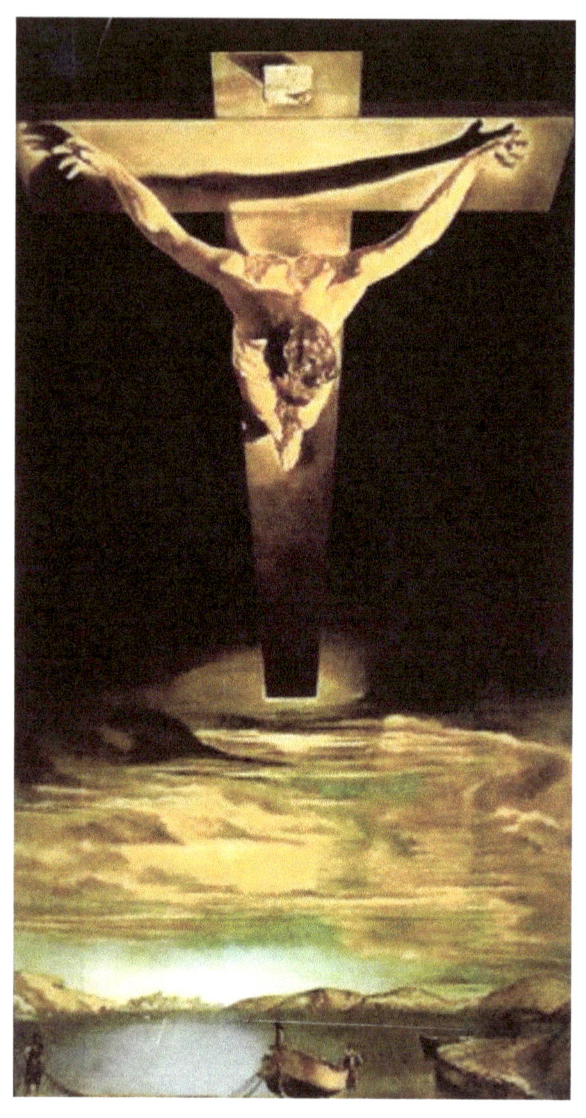

Crucifixion

Facts for Life – Part 1

The Fact of Creation
"In the beginning God made the heavens and the earth" -
Genesis 1:1
The Fact of the Creation of Humankind
God created man in his own image, in the image of God he
created them; male and female he created them - *Genesis
1:27*
The Fact of the Goodness of Creation
God saw all that he had made, and it was very good -
Genesis 1:31
The Fact of the Garden of Eden
The Lord God took the man and put him in the Garden of
Eden, to work it and take care of it - *Genesis 2:15*
The Fact of God's Command to Humankind
The Lord God commanded the man, "You are free to eat
from any tree in the garden; but you must not eat from the
tree of the knowledge of good and evil, for when you eat of
it you will surely die" - *Genesis 2:16*
The Fact of the Temptation of Humankind
The serpent (identified as Satan) said to the woman, "You
will not surely die. For God knows that when you eat of it
your eyes will be opened, and you will be like God, knowing
good and evil" - *Genesis 3:4,5*
The Fact of the Fall of Humankind
When the woman saw that the fruit of the tree was good for
food and pleasing to the eye, and also desirable for gaining
wisdom, she took some and ate it. She also gave some to
her husband, who was with her, and he ate it - *Genesis 3:6*
The Fact of Humankind's Excuses for Disobedience
God said to the man, "Have you eaten from the tree that I
commanded you not to eat from?" The man said, "The
woman you put here with me – she gave me some fruit from

the tree and I ate it." Then the Lord said to the woman, "What is this that you have done?" The woman said, "The serpent deceived me and I ate" - *Genesis 3:2,13*

The Fact of God's Judgment

The Lord God said to the serpent, "Because you have done this…I will put enmity between you and the woman, and between your offspring and hers; he will crush your head, and you will bruise his heel." So the Lord God banished humankind from the Garden of Eden to work the ground from which they had been taken - *Genesis 3:14,15 and 23*

The Fact of Evil – the Fall of Satan and His Angels

There was war in heaven. Michael and his angels fought against the dragon, and the dragon and his angels fought back. But he was not strong enough, and they lost their place in heaven. The great dragon was hurled down, that ancient serpent called the devil, or Satan, who leads the whole world astray.   He was hurled to the earth, and his angels with him - *Revelation 12:7 – 9*

The Fact of Satan's Nature and Activities in the World

As Satan tempted and succeeded in deceiving humankind in the Garden of Eden, so he tempted Jesus in the desert. However, he failed to deceive Jesus who countered his lies with the truth of the Word of God, "It is written" - *Matthew 4:1-11*

Jesus describes Satan as 'the god of this world, a liar and the father of lies.' - *John 8:44*

An adversary who prowls around like a roaring lion seeking someone to devour - *1 Peter 5:8*

The Fact of the Need for Repentance

Repentance is to turn away from sins. It is a change of mind that results in a change of action. "If you repent, I will restore you that you may serve me" - *Jeremiah 15:19*

"Repent then, and turn to God, so that your sins may be wiped out" - *Acts 3:19*
Jesus said, "Repent and believe the gospel": *Mark 1:15*

The Fact of the Good News of the Gospel
"Now brothers, I want to remind you of the gospel I preached to you, which you received and on which you have taken your stand. By this gospel you are saved if you hold firmly to the word I preached to you. Otherwise you have believed in vain. For what I received I passed on to you as of first importance; that Christ died for our sins according to the Scriptures, that he was buried, that he was raised on the third day according to the Scriptures – "For as in Adam all die, so in Christ shall all be made alive" - *1 Corinthians 15: 1-3 and 22*

The Fact of the Victory of the Cross of Christ
"When you were dead in your sins and in the un-circumcision of your sinful nature, God made you alive with Christ. He forgave all our sins, having cancelled the written code with its regulations, that was against us and that stood opposed to us; he took it away, nailing it to the cross. And having made a public spectacle of them, triumphing over them by the cross" - *Colossians 2:13*

Facts for Life – Part 2

The Fact of Jesus Christ the Only Way to God

"There is no other name under heaven given among men whereby we must be saved" - *Acts 4:12*

Jesus said, "I am the Way, the Truth, and the Life. No one can come to the Father except through me" - *John 14:6*

"He was wounded for our transgressions; he was bruised for our iniquities, the chastisement for our peace was upon him, and by his stripes we are healed. All we like sheep have gone astray; we have turned every one to his own way; and the Lord has laid on him the iniquity of us all" - *Isaiah 53:5,6*

"He himself bore our sins in his body on the tree, so that we might die to sins and live for righteousness; by his wounds you have been healed" - 1 *Peter 2:24*

John the Baptist said, "Behold the Lamb of God, who takes away the sin of the world." - *John1:29*

The Apostle Paul said, "I have been crucified with Christ, it is no longer I who live but Christ who lives in me. The life I now live in the flesh I live by faith in the Son of God, who loved me and gave himself for me." - *Galatians 2:20*

The Fact of the Second Coming of Christ

The Ascension: He was taken up before their very eyes, and a cloud hid him from their sight. They were looking intently up into the sky as he was going, when suddenly two men dressed in white stood beside them. "Men of Galilee", they said, "Why do you stand here looking into the sky?   This same Jesus, who has been taken from you into heaven, will come back in the same way you have seen him go into heaven" - *Acts 1:9-11*

Now, brothers, about times and dates we do not need to write to you, for you know very well that the day of the Lord will come like a thief in the night. While people are saying, "Peace and safety", destruction will come on them suddenly,

as labour pains on a pregnant woman, and they will not escape - 1 *Thessalonians 5:1-3.* Look, he is coming with the clouds, and every eye will see him, even those who pierced him; and all the peoples of the earth will mourn because of him. So shall it be! Amen - *Revelation 1:7*
You also must be ready, because the Son of Man will come at an hour when you do not expect him - *Luke 12:40*
For the Lord himself will come down from heaven, with a loud command, with the voice of the archangel and with the trumpet call of God - *Thessalonians 4:16*
At that time the sign of the Son of Man will appear in the sky, and all the nations of the earth will mourn. They will see the Son of Man coming on the clouds of the sky, with power and great glory. And he will send his angels with a loud trumpet call, and they will gather his elect from the four winds, from one end of the heavens to the other - *Matthew 24:30*

The Fact of the Final Judgment

"For all have sinned and fall short of the glory of God" - *Romans 2:23*
"There is none that does good, not even one" - *Psalm 14:3*
Jesus said, "Whoever commits sin is the slave of sin" - *John 8:34*
"We must all appear before the judgment seat of Christ, to receive what has been done in the body, whether good or bad" - *2 Corinthians 5:10*
The sheep and the goats. "When the Son of Man comes in his glory, and all his angels with him, he will sit on his throne in the heavenly glory. All the nations will be gathered before him, and he will separate the people from one another as a shepherd separates the sheep from the goats. He will put the sheep on his right hand and the goats on his left. Then he will say to those on his left - "Depart from me, you who are

cursed into the eternal fire prepared for the devil and his angels" - *Matthew 25:31*

"He said to me, it is done. I am the Alpha and Omega, the Beginning and the End. To him who is thirsty I will give to drink without cost from the spring of the water of life. He who overcomes will inherit all this, and I will be his God and he will be my son. But the cowardly, the unbelieving, the vile, the sexually immoral, those who practise magic arts, the idolaters and all liars, their place will be in the fiery lake of burning sulphur. This is the second death. - *Revelation 21:6-8*

"Not everyone who says to me, 'Lord, Lord' will enter the kingdom pf heaven, but the one who does the will of my Father who is in heaven. On that day many will come and say to me, 'Lord, Lord, did we not prophesy in your name, and cast out demons in your name, and do mighty works in your name?' And then I will declare to them, I never knew you; depart from me, you workers of lawlessness." - *Matthew 7:21-23*

The Fact of the Truth of Scripture

"All Scripture is inspired by God and profitable for teaching, for reproof, for correction, for training in righteousness; so that the man of God may be adequate, equipped for every good work" - *2 Timothy 3:16,17*

"For the word of the Lord is right and true; he is faithful in all he does" - *Psalm 33:4*

Sanctify them in the truth; your word is truth - *John 17:17*

"Your word is a lamp to my feet and a light to, my path" - *Psalm 119:105*

"This is the word of the Lord."   *"Thanks be to God"*

Faith

The keyword is 'Faith'. "the righteous will live by his faith" – *Habakkuk 2:4*. In the Apostle Paul's second letter to Timothy, he refers to Timothy's "sincere faith", which it seems he learned from his mother and grandmother. In the Gospel of Luke chapter 17 verse 5, the Apostles said to the Lord – "increase our faith". It is a strange fact that in the Old Testament the word 'faith' is found only twice, in Deuteronomy 32:20, and in Habakkuk 2:4, but in the New Testament it occurs more than 240 times. This does not mean that faith is unimportant in the Old Testament, because the idea, if not the word, is frequent, and is usually expressed by words such as believe, trust and hope.

So what is faith? Have we got it, what use is it, and what do we do with it? It is a fact that everyone has faith of some kind, because without it, life would be impossible. Every day we entrust ourselves to some thing or person, without consciously realising it. What is Christian faith and how does it differ from common human faith? Does it consist of some vague woolly notion about the goodness of God? Is it hoping for the best, a sort of stoical gritting of teeth in the face of desperate circumstances? Is it 'pie in the sky when we die', or is it more substantial than that? The writer of the letter to the Hebrews chapter 11 verse 1, describes Christian faith like this – "Now faith is being sure of what we hope for, and certain of what we do not see." Nothing vague or woolly, no wishful thinking, but something very positive and decisive.

Thankfully, our relationship with God does not depend on the strength or weakness of our faith, but upon the reliability and faithfulness of God, the faithful Creator, who cannot lie and always keeps His promises. We believe in what He is, and in what He has said and done. It is not blind faith, but firmly based on the evidence of our own personal experience, the witness of countless Christians down through the ages, and the accounts of God's dealings with both Jews and Gentiles as recorded in the Bible. It is firmly rooted in the reality of people, places and history, and not in fantasy. That is why it can be describes as sure and certain. But the evidence cannot be expressed in visual terms, because that would destroy the whole idea of faith and trust, which is being certain of things we do not see. As the Apostle Paul says in his second letter to the Corinthians chapter 5 verse 7 – "We live by faith and not by sight". Even though the Apostles had the visual evidence of the person of Jesus with them, and what He was saying and doing, they became aware that their faith was weak, because their minds could not grasp the eternal truths He was demonstrating among them. So they said to Him – "Increase out faith". The response of Jesus goes much deeper than a superficial direct answer to their request – "If you have faith as small as a mustard seed, you can say to this mulberry tree, be uprooted and planted in the sea, and it will obey you. Matthew records that on another occasion He said – "You can say to this mountain, move from here to there, and it will move. Nothing will be impossible for you". Hence the expression "faith can move mountains". We understand that Jesus was not being literal here, but teaching that by faith, seemingly impossible problems and obstacles can be solved and overcome. It's not the quantity, but the quality of faith that is required. Faith as small as a mustard seed, but which is capable of growing into a large plant or tree.

So, being assured that we have faith, no matter how small; of what use is it? What we believe must affect what we do. If we believe that a bus will take us to where we want to go, then by faith we board the bus. Our action perfects our faith, and makes it real. That is why the Bible says that faith without actions is dead. The Nicene Creed is a statement of our faith, what we believe as Christians, and we must act according to what we say we believe, especially in relation to our Lord Jesus Christ, His death and resurrection, His teaching and commands. Politicians have a creed or statement of beliefs as set out in their manifestos, and discussed with energy, enthusiasm and passion at their annual party conferences. We believe in fairer distribution of wealth, or we believe in privatisation of national industries, or we believe in the proportional representation voting system. These are important issues affecting us all, but they don't have eternal consequences. How much more then, should Christians speak with energy, enthusiasm and passion about our statement of belief, the one true message of reconciliation between God and humankind, the message of salvation to a lost and dying world. Time is perhaps running out as we expect the return of our Lord to reclaim His kingdom. We do not know when that will be, but we are to be aware of the signs of the times, and to be ready for 'that day'. The Church is perceived as being in decline in the West, and its moral authority weakened. There are ominous portents such as global warming, relentless destruction of the world's forests, the increasing size of the hole in the ozone layer, global pandemics, collapse of financial systems affecting world trade.

Our Lord Jesus gave only two commands to His followers – love one another, and go and make disciples of all nations. It is time to put faith into action, not to draw back in fear. The Apostle Paul says to Timothy and so to us – "God has not given us a spirit of timidity, but a spirit of power, of love and self-discipline", and exhorts him and us to be "not ashamed to testify about our Lord". Away with doubt and fear, and as good Christian soldiers, let us put on the whole armour of God, especially the shield of faith. Faith is being sure of what we hope for, and certain of what we do not see.

Forgive Us Our Sins

The prayer we know as the Lord's Prayer was given in response to the disciples' request, "Lord, teach us to pray." It rewards study because it contains all the elements we need for a healthy and fruitful prayer life. Here we are looking at the petition, "Forgive us our sins, as we forgive those who sin against us." 'Sin' is a nasty little word, and one that we don't like to hear. It's like a snake hissing; something you spit out because you don't like the taste of it. Sin is at the heart of everything that is wrong in the world; a disease that brings horror and death and destruction in its wake. If sin is the disease, sins are its symptoms, and it is spiritually terminal unless dealt with and healed. If we refuse to admit that we are sick, then we won't seek healing, and the healing that is needed is forgiveness. That healing has already been provided for us by our Lord Jesus in His sacrificial death on the cross. The words of the well known hymn describe this very well, "He died that we might be forgiven, He died to make us good, that we might go at last to heaven, saved by His precious blood." He dealt there fully and eternally with the effects of the disease and the symptoms, and as believers we are counted as righteous and whole before God. However, the virus is still active in the world and will attack and weaken us if we stray away from the physician of souls. It cannot destroy us, but will render us less effective in the spiritual battle in which we are engaged. Awareness of it will cause us to seek after deliverance and healing. Confession is the means by which this is achieved, because admission of the truth of our condition is made, and the healing balm of forgiveness is allowed to be applied.

Healing and cleansing are synonymous in the Scriptures. If we confess our sins, we are cleansed from all unrighteousness, restored and made whole; fit again for service. King David discovered the truth of this. He says, "When I kept silent, my bones wasted away through my groaning all the day long. Then I acknowledged my sin to you, and did not cover up my iniquity. I said, I will confess my transgressions to the Lord, and you forgave the the guilt of my sin." - *Psalm 32:3.* Nothing is more debilitating than guilt, the cause of much of the mental illness in our society. We don't need to carry it around. Confession will unload that intolerable burden and set us free. We say, "forgive us our sins", but the petition goes on, "as we forgive those who sin against us." Forgiveness appears to be conditional. In this petition we are asking God to deal with us in the same way as we deal with others. If we are living in an unforgiving spirit towards other people, in effect in this petition, we are asking God not to forgive us! It is a hard saying. The question arises; should we forgive those who sin against us if they will not admit to having offended? The answer must surely be, yes! Our heavenly Father's forgiveness is conditional upon our forgiving others. It only becomes a reality in our experience when we repent and accept it. So we are called to forgive others unconditionally, and to go on doing it. When the Apostle Peter asked the Lord, "how many times shall I forgive my brother when he sins against me? Up to seven times?" Jesus replied – "I tell you, not seven times, but seventy seven times." In other words, without limit. The consequences for us if we don't is that we ourselves can't receive forgiveness from God. It's not that He is unwilling to give it, but we have created a blockage where we can't receive it; imprisoned by our own unforgiving spirit. But we find, humanly speaking, sometimes it is impossible to forgive; the hurt and the wounds are too deep and too painful. We want revenge; demand the head on the plate. What are we to do? Like the Apostle Paul, we know what we should do, but find we can't do it. We are told to love our enemies, to do good to those who use us badly, but we can't do it. Can Jews forgive the Holocaust? Can Bosnian Moslems forgive Serbs? Can Protestants and Catholics forgive each other in Northern Ireland? It is only the power of the Holy Spirit that enables us to forgive. It was our sins that nailed our Lord Jesus to the cross, and thrust the spear through His side. What was His response? "Father forgive them; they don't know what they are doing." Let this mind be in us which was in Christ Jesus. There is no other way than forgiveness from the heart.

Having been forgiven and having forgiven anyone who has sinned against us, something else is needful; to learn to forgive ourselves which is the secret of inner peace. Self hate is destructive and is a form of spiritual pride. The temptation to dwell on failure, and keep asking ourselves how we could have done such a thing. So, for healthy and effective Christian living, these are the things we should bear in mind -:

1. Confess our sins. Not morbid soul searching, but asking the Holy Spirit to search our hearts.
2. Forgive those who sin against us.
3. Accept God's forgiveness.
4. Forgive ourselves.

Consider Him who poured out His soul to death. He bore the sin of many and made intercession for the transgressors. It is only when we consider the debt we owe to Christ that we shall fully appreciate why we must forgive.

Harvest Thanksgiving

"Man does not live on bread alone, but on every word that comes from the mouth of God." *Deuteronomy 8: 3.*

At Harvest time we celebrate and give thanks to God for His bounteous provision for us, and especially for the food we eat. We think about and marvel at the wonder of Creation, the infinite variety of the things our loving Father has made. So we sing, "All good things around us are sent from heaven above, then thank the Lord, O thank the Lord, for all His love." The basic things we need to survive are bread and water, and these two figure very strongly in the Scriptures. In some parts of the world in conditions of famine and drought, even these essentials are not available. So aid is sought from more affluent countries, where there are enough of this world's goods. Christians are at the forefront in providing such relief, through charities such as Christian Aid and Tear Fund. There are millions starving in the world today, but even if we could feed them all, we have not given them all they need. We feed our bodies every day to keep them fit and healthy, and we feed our minds with knowledge to improve the quality of our lives and bring fulfilment. But there is another dimension which needs feeding, and which we ignore at our peril. We are body, mind and spirit, and it is the unseen part of our make-up which tends to be neglected. Materialistic society rejects the need for true spiritual food, and is blind to the poverty this brings to human life. But sooner or later, the spirit demands to be satisfied and cannot be ignored. The deep seated hunger is there even if not recognised, and a quest begins to bring relief and fill the void. This quest can travel many roads, some dead ends, circular routes, some pitfalls, but if followed with determination, can lead to the true source of life which Christians have found in our Lord and Saviour,

Jesus Christ. Humankind cannot live on bread alone. The spiritual part of our humanity is in fact far more important, because it is eternal. The rest is subject to decay and rots away. The body and mind needs daily intake of food and knowledge to grow to maturity, and so does the spirit, if we are not to become unbalanced and less than whole.

Where then, is the spiritual food we need? Our Lord Jesus has the answer, or more accurately, is the answer, because He says, "I am the bread of life. If anyone eats this bread, he will live forever. The bread of God is that bread which comes down from heaven, and gives life to the world." Symbolically, we partake of this heavenly bread in the celebration of the Eucharist, the body and blood of our Lord Jesus. He alone can satisfy our spiritual hunger and thirst. Did He not say to the Samaritan woman who He met at Jacob's Well, "Everyone who drinks this water will be thirsty again, but whoever drinks the water I give him will become in him a spring of water welling up to eternal life." Here is the eternal dimension again, symbolised in both bread and water.

The neglect of the spiritual dimension in our society is all too plain to see. We can be physically and materially rich, yet spiritually and morally bankrupt. Our daily newspapers and TV screens, and our own hearts, reveal the truth of our condition. The Church is seeking to redress this imbalance, but the Church itself needs to be renewed if it is to be effective in its appointed commission to, "Go and make disciples of all nations." In the Revelation to John we read that the church at Laodicea was taken to task by the Holy Spirit, "You say, 'I am rich; I have acquired wealth and do not need a thing'. But you do not realise that you are wretched, pitiful, poor, blind and naked." This is the complacent, self satisfied church, that leaves its Lord standing outside the door, knocking to come in. So be earnest and repent, says the Lord, "Here I am! I stand at the door and knock. If anyone hears my voice and opens the door, I will come in and eat with him, and he with me." There is no room for complacency in the Church. The fields are white for the harvest but the labourers are few. So what can we do to reverse the progress of spiritual famine? We must start where we are, with ourselves. Individually we may be insignificant, but a forest canopy is made up of millions of individual leaves, all of equal value and contributing to the glory and wonder of the whole. Be assured that we belong to Christ, not because of how good we are, or think we are, but because of what He has done for us.

Desire communion with Him, a closer walk, by daily reading and study of the Bible, prayer and obedience to His revealed will. The closer we are to Him, the more conformed we will become to His nature, reaching out in love and compassion to others, to the poor, the lonely and the lost sheep. This is how we grow spiritually, just as we partake of daily food to grow and mature physically. So today, let us rejoice and give thanks to our Father God, for all that He has given us richly to enjoy, our food, clothing, shelter, family and friends. But above all, for the bread which comes down from heaven and gives life to the world, our Lord and Saviour, Jesus Christ. Let us feed on Him by faith with thanksgiving. "Man does not live by bread alone, but by every word that comes from the mouth of the Lord." *Matthew 4:4*

I Am the True Vine

The words 'I am', are significant in Scripture. Our Lord's use of the words, are on the face of it, innocent enough, but they drove the Jews wild with anger. This comes out clearly in *John 8:58* when, at the conclusion of a discourse about Abraham, He says to them, "Truly, truly, I say to you, before Abraham was, I am." For the true significance of this we need to refer to *Exodus 3:13,14.* Moses said to God - "If I come to the people of Israel and say to them, 'The God of your fathers has sent me to you,' and they ask me, 'What is his name?' What shall I say to them?" God said to Moses, "I AM WHO I AM". Say to the people of Israel, 'I AM has sent me to you.' No wonder the Jews took up stones to throw at Him.

Today we are looking at this saying of our Lord Jesus, "I am the True Vine." The grapevine is mentioned throughout Scripture, and frequently in a symbolic sense. It is first named in *Genesis 9:20*, when Noah planted a vineyard and produced wine from it. It was also cultivated in ancient Egypt. The vine was the emblem of prosperity and peace among the ancient Hebrews. More particularly it symbolised the chosen people. They were the vine which God had taken out of Egypt. In *Isaiah 5:1–7,* we read the sad little song of the vineyard, carefully cared for by the owner, but when he looked for it to yield grapes, it yielded wild grapes. The vineyard of the Lord of Hosts is the House of Israel. So we see the symbolism of the vineyard. It is the people of God, and the Lord of Hosts is the owner, who tends and cares for it, watches over it, to see that it produces the fruit that He intended it to produce. Through the prophet Isaiah, God asks the question, "When I looked for it to yield grapes, why did it yield wild grapes?" The question is not directly answered, and we need to look beyond the symbolic vine to the people themselves, the House of Israel. "For the vineyard of the Lord of Hosts is the House of Israel, and the men of Judah are His pleasant planting; and He looked for justice, but behold, bloodshed; for righteousness, but behold, a cry" - *Isaiah 5:7*. The vineyard is diseased, and the disease is sin, as the rest of Isaiah chapter 5 makes clear. But then, into this diseased vineyard, in due time, and according to the design and purpose of the owner, a new vine is planted and grows to produce the fruit that God intended. Our Lord Jesus is that vine, the true vine of which the vine of Israel is but the type. As we read in *John 15,* "Jesus said, I am the true vine, and my Father is the gardener."

The purpose of any vine is to bear fruit, and so the vine cannot be considered apart from its fruit bearing branches. "I am the vine, you are the branches", says our Lord Jesus. He is the true vine with whom all true believers are in organic relationship. The gardener, the vinedresser, tends and cares for His vine by feeding it, watching over it, and pruning the branches. A completely fruitless branch is not worthy of the vine because it cannot be drawing sap from the main stem. The word branch is commonly used in connection with organisations and associations meaning parts or groups attached to the main controlling authority or headquarters. Our Lord Jesus says to His followers, "Abide in me, and I in you." The branch can receive no sap from the vine unless there is constant and unimpeded contact between them. Jesus brings out the principle of the utter dependence of His disciples upon Him. Those not abiding in the vine are not essentially a part of the vine, and are cut off from its life.

If we look at our Lord's words in *John 15,* He draws out some important truths for us. In verse 7 we see that abiding in Him gives assurance of answered prayer, because those who abide will desire to do the Father's will. In verse 8 we see that fruit bearing is not an end in itself; its purpose is that the Father will be glorified. In verse 16 we see that we have been chosen to go and bear fruit that will last. And finally, in verse 17, we see the fruit of the vine summed up in a single word – Love. Jesus said to His disciples, "This is my command, love one another." That fruit of love can only be produced by abiding in the vine whose name is Love. In his letter to the Galatians chapter 5 verse 14, the Apostle Paul says - "The entire law is summed up in a single command - love your neighbour as yourself." He goes on to list the fruit of the Spirit, beginning with love, then joy, peace, patience, kindness, goodness, faithfulness, gentleness, and self control. If we are branches attached to the vine and drawing our supplies from Him alone, then no matter what we call ourselves, no matter how we are called to serve and to worship, we shall produce fruit that will last. Fruit which we were intended to produce and for which we were created. And all this to the end that in all things, our gracious and loving God and Father will be glorified.

True Vine

Importance of Preparation

When I was conscripted into the army at age 18, it was made clear to us raw recruits, barely just out of school, that we were not paid to think, but to do as we were told. The simple rule of thumb principle of army life was summed up in these words, "If it moves, salute it; if it doesn't move, paint it." Some of life's rich lessons are not easily forgotten! Something everyone who has ever painted anything should know, is the vital importance of preparation, before the finish is applied. Careful rubbing down, filling, undercoating, before the gloss coat goes on. Any newly painted surface will look good for a while, but what has been done or not done underneath, will eventually become apparent. Prepare means to make ready or suitable in advance for some use or event. We prepare for Christmas, for our family, the arrival of guests, make ready to receive them. A recurring nightmare for hosts is that guests arrive, and nothing is ready, everything in chaos! Proper and adequate preparation is necessary for anything worthwhile. The season of Advent is a time of expectation and preparation as we look forward to the celebration of the birth of our Lord Jesus Christ. Our richest enjoyment of that time will depend to a very large extent on the quality of our preparation. Advent carols, church services, reading the Gospel accounts of the events surrounding the birth of our Lord, the significance of His incarnation, the wonder and beauty of it all. Pondering all these things in our hearts, as Mary did. Preparation for the day when we welcome Him, joining the shepherds and angels in worship and songs of praise. Advent is the time when we think about the one sent by God to prepare the way of the Lord. The one foretold by the prophet Isaiah, and about whom it is written, "I will send my messenger ahead of you, who will prepare your way before you." And so John came prophesying in the desert region, and preaching a baptism of repentance.

Think about John the Baptist and consider what we can learn from him. He was the vital and necessary preparation for the appearance of the Messiah, the Christ, the Son of God. What do we know about John the Baptist? His birth was the answer to the prayers of godly but ageing parents, Zechariah and Elizabeth (a cousin of the Virgin Mary). The angel told Zechariah what his name should be, "You are to give him the name John", and that he would go on before the Lord in the spirit and power of Elijah, to make ready a people prepared for the Lord. John lived in the desert until he appeared publicly to Israel. He was recognised as a prophet, and some thought he could be the Christ. He said to them, "I am not the Christ, but am sent ahead of Him." He was not the light, but came to bear witness to the light. When Jesus came to John to be baptised in the River Jordan, it was revealed to John that this was the Son of God, and he testified, "Look, the Lamb of God, who takes away the sin of the world." John was the last and greatest of all the prophets. Our Lord said of him, "Among those born of women there has not arisen anyone greater than John the Baptist." When Jesus appeared, the work of John was finished. John recognised this when he said, "He must increase; I must decrease." His life ended in prison, put to death by Herod, tricked by Herodias and Salome.

We who belong to Christ, through faith and trust in His redeeming blood, are called by God to do some work with Him. No matter how small the task, there are things that only we can do as unique individuals loved by God, and which no one else can do. He gives us the power to do it by His indwelling and outpouring Spirit. We are called to testify with John - "I have seen and testify that this is the Son of God."

At times, we may have doubts, but as part of the body of Christ, we must return to the one who made the blind to see, the lame to walk, the deaf to hear, who raised the dead, and preached good news to the poor. As we consider any possible alternatives, we are driven back, as the disciples were, to the conclusion; "To whom shall we go? You have the words of eternal life." As we see our role in making way for the Son of God, we realise that we too must decrease, and He must increase. Just as an undercoat is covered and lost to sight when the final gloss coat is applied. What we desire is that our Lord Jesus Christ is clearly seen in all His beauty and glory, and that all the praise goes to Him. John the Baptist prepared the way of the Lord, and his preparation was powerful and effective. It is written that, "People, even tax collectors, when they heard Jesus' words, acknowledged that God's way was right, because they had been baptised by John." But the Pharisees, and the experts in the law, rejected God's purpose for them, because they had not been baptised by John.

Our Lord Jesus allowed Himself to be the sacrificial victim for our sakes. The preparation had been laid by the Father from the beginning, through Abraham, the people of Israel, and all the prophets, until John the Baptist. All the preparation and conditions were now perfect for the completion of the work of redemption, the miraculous healing ministry of our Lord Jesus Christ, the preaching of the good news of the kingdom of God, and culminating in the triumphant cry from the cross, "It is finished!" Let us then prepare a place for Him in our homes, in our hearts, and in our lives; in everything we do. For He has gone to the Father's house to prepare a place for us. Amen!

In the Beginning

"In the beginning". Two books of the Bible start with these words; the first book of the Old Testament, Genesis, and the fourth Gospel of the New Testament, according to John. About 1400 years separate the writers, Moses and John, but each speaks about the Creator and the Creation. The first tells of the sequence of creation, and how God saw everything that He had made and that it was good. The second tells of the Word who was with God and who was God, and through whom all things were made. Both writers refer to the Spirit of God who was moving over the face of the waters, and who descended on the Word made flesh, at His baptism in the River Jordan. The testimony is the same, in the beginning there was God, and He created the heavens and the earth and everything in it.

A jet engine is a wonderful piece of engineering, and it seems like a miracle that thousands of tons of metal can take off from the ground and fly through the air. Imagine someone who had never seen an aeroplane before asks the question – "Who designed and made this wonderful machine?", and receives the answer – "No one designed and made it. It all came together on its own, and no one knows how!" Would anyone with the slightest intelligence accept that explanation? Yet that is what atheists and humanists maintain is how our world, indeed the whole universe, which is infinitely more complex than a jet aeroplane, came together, purely by chance! It seems to me that you need an awful lot of faith to be an atheist!   Is it any wonder then, that the Scripture says – "the fool has said in his heart, there is no God." The Scripture also says that what can be known about God is plain to humankind, because He has shown it to them. "Ever since the creation of the world His invisible nature, namely His eternal power and deity, has been clearly perceived in the things that have been made. So they are without excuse."- *Romans 1:20*. There is no excuse for atheism. In fact, the majority of people do claim to believe in a Creator, but they choose to ignore Him, and pretend that they do not need Him. They are as blind as atheists, and are described by the Apostle Paul like this - "They exchanged the truth about God for a lie, and worshipped and served the creature rather than the Creator."

God speaks to us through His creation. The infinite variety, wonder and beauty of created things are clear evidence of a mighty and loving God. The tenderness with which animals care for and protect their young reflects the tenderness and protective care of the Creator. The beauty of plants and flowers which soon fade and die, shows the loving detail God lavishes on such transient things, and all for us to enjoy. Yet we do not trust Him to care for us, His greatest creation! We struggle and strive to live independently of Him, the One in whom we live and move and have our being. It is madness and the consequence of sin. The reason for all the chaos and misery in the world is that we have turned every one to his own way, everyone doing what is right in his own eyes. We make our own moral laws to suit ourselves. In the words of the Apostle Paul - "We know the whole creation has been groaning as in the pain of childbirth up to the present time." - *Romans 8:22.* But it will eventually "be set free from its bondage to decay." - *Romans 8:21*

Salt is used to prevent decay.   Christians are described as "the salt of the earth". The prayers and influence of the saints, not a select few super Christians, keep the forces of evil in check. Spiritual decline is the main cause of decay and moral decadence, and ultimately brings a nation to ruin. We need Christian leaders and standards in every area of life; those who acknowledge the Creator God and who seek to walk in His ways. There are forces at work which are led by the spirit of anti-Christ. Beware of anything that denies the Creator and seeks to put substitutes in His place. Anything that puts emphasis on self-awareness, self-reliance, searching within for truth, looking to the earth or the stars for answers, playing around with spiritualism, astrology, palm reading, tarot cards and the like, can lead to bondage in occult practices. We should be concerned about abuse of the trust God has placed in us in having control of the planet He has given us. We should bring pressure to bear wherever possible to promote the physical health and welfare of people and their environment. But this is not our prime concern. We are called to be lights in the world, to point people to the Creator God who loves them, and to His Son who died for them, that they might live forever with Him. This world is not our final home. We look to a new heaven and a new earth, to the holy city, the new Jerusalem, where our Lord has gone to prepare a place for us, and where we shall live with Him in the presence of our God forever.

Jacob

The home life of Jacob, the second born of the twin sons of Isaac and Rebekah, could hardly be described as a happy one! Jacob was very much controlled by his mother and did what she told him. The Scripture says that Isaac loved Esau, the firstborn, and Rebekah loved Jacob. Such division and favouritism within a family, and not least within the family of the Church, can be a recipe for disaster. Rebekah persuaded Jacob to deceive his blind father and obtain the blessing which rightly belonged to the firstborn son. So Jacob stole the blessing which, according to family law, once given could not be revoked. When Esau found out, naturally he was furious and threatened to kill Jacob. But Esau had been careless about his birth-right and on one occasion had been willing to sell it to Jacob in exchange for a good meal. At his mother's instigation, and with his father's blessing, Jacob left his home, and in fear of his brother's vengeance, set out to find a wife from the family of his mother's brother. On the way he stopped for the night and had a dream or vision in which God gave him the same promise he had made to his grandfather Abraham, and to his father Isaac, that all the peoples on earth would be blessed through them and their offspring.

Now fast forward to Genesis 32 where we see Jacob with his two wives, Leah and Rachel, and their eleven sons. He is reaching another crisis point in his life, struggling in his mind with the constant threat of his brother's revenge, and with God's amazing promise about his future. One night, and in this state of mind, he was challenged to physical combat by an unnamed man who wrestled with him until daybreak. Perhaps this was symbolic of what was going on in his head. In this contest it seems that Jacob's underlying nature and resolve were being tested to the limit, and resulted in his hip being put out of joint. He recognised that his opponent was none other than an angel of God, from whom Jacob insisted on obtaining a blessing before he would let him go. A far greater blessing than he had stolen from his father, and what he received was a changed character and a new name.

Normal reasoning adults, responsible for their actions under the law, are not entirely the result of their upbringing and environment. We are not manipulated puppets but responsible to God for what we do. But whatever our circumstances we can be changed as we freely enter into a personal relationship with God through faith in Jesus Christ. We are offered the promise of his presence with us, his forgiveness, and life beyond the grave. We believe in a God of wholeness and healing who is able to heal past memories and hurts; environmental issues such as physical and sexual abuse, alcohol and drug abuse. For many, born into poverty and deprivation, these are serious, damaging and often overwhelming problems. But God's justice is seen in the words of our Lord according to Luke to privileged people like you and me, "to whom much is given, much will be required." The story of Jacob should be an encouragement to us. All God's promises to him have been fulfilled through imperfect Israel, and the emergence of the Messiah, the Christ, through whom all peoples on earth will be blessed. The ultimate fulfilment of the promise to Jacob will be when our Lord Jesus Christ comes again in glory to judge the world in righteousness. Then we shall see the healing of the nations and there will be no more death or mourning or crying or pain anymore. But for us, here and now, we can take our comfort from the transforming and healing power of God in Christ, and the fact that, whatever our circumstances, we are fully known and loved by the God of Abraham, the God of Isaac, and the God of Jacob.

Jesus Friend of Sinners

What is a friend? A friend has been described as someone who knows all about you, but loves you just the same. Do you have a friend like that? The truth is we cannot know anyone completely. We cannot even know ourselves completely. But there are things we do know about ourselves we wouldn't want even our best friend to know. We are all defensive to a degree, and hide behind masks, because we are sinners and are ashamed. Our first parents hid from the presence of God in shame when they realised they had disobeyed Him, and covered themselves up, lest their nakedness should be exposed. Before that, they were innocent, open and unashamed. What people see of us is not all there is, and we go to some lengths to ensure that what is seen is the best side of our character and appearance. It is therefore difficult for us to be truly ourselves. A certain degree of reticence is necessary if we are to live happily with our neighbours. If we went around telling everyone we met about all our faults, we would soon be written off as bores at best, and mentally unstable at worst. So there is a compromise we must live with in a civilised society.

Fortunately for us, there is someone who does know all about us, but loves us just the same. Jesus Christ our Saviour, fully identified Himself with our humanity, was in all points tempted as we are, and understands us completely. King David, the psalmist, knew this truth about God, when he wrote what we know as Psalm 139, - "O Lord, you have searched me and know me. You know when I sit and when I rise; you perceive my thoughts from afar. You discern my going out and my lying down; you are familiar with all my ways. Before a word is on my tongue you know it completely O Lord." There is nowhere we can go, nothing we can say, or do, or think, that is hidden from God. It's not like '1984' by George Orwell, 'Big Brother is watching you', but the one who sees and knows us, loves and cares, and wants only the best for us. We should not want to hurt or disappoint such a friend. Our Lord Jesus is one in whom we can confide, to whom we can speak openly and honestly about anything. He knows all about it, and the situation is already under His control if we will hand it to him, and allow Him to have His way. He has a plan and purpose for each one of us, but which requires our co-operation to fulfil it in the best possible way. Unfortunately, we rebel and want to go our own way. But with infinite love and patience, He guides us back as we learn from our errors and disobedience. The wonderful promise is that in spite of our wilful ways, one day He will present us without fault before the Father. We cannot imagine that, but we can claim the promise of Romans 8 -"Therefore there is now no condemnation to those who are in Christ Jesus." If we truly belong to Christ and live according to the Spirit, we are one with Him, part of His body, the Church, and therefore share His perfection and inheritance. What a Friend and Saviour we have, who identifies with us so fully and completely.

The teachers of the law, the Pharisees, were very jealous of Jesus and what He was doing among the people, and the following He seemed to have. They were always trying to catch Him out, to be able to accuse Him of some error in His teaching or His actions. The question 'why' was always on their lips, "why does He eat with tax collectors and sinners?" they asked His disciples. Jesus answered them, "It is not the healthy who need a doctor but the sick. I have not come to call the righteous but sinners."   Yes, we are all sinners, but counted righteous in God's sight because our righteousness comes through faith in Jesus Christ, to all who believe. No matter how healthy or wealthy people may appear, apart from Jesus they are sick and in need of healing, even if they don't know it. There are people who know they are sick, the lonely, the outcasts of society, those who are despised. They need help, but don't know where to turn. They need a friend they can trust, to love and care for them. We who believe and trust in Jesus have found such a Friend, who calls upon us to befriend those who need Him. It is perhaps more in our actions than our words that people recognise the love of Jesus.

Jesus the Friend of sinners. People need such a Friend who will never turn away, but will always be with them. There was a time, many years ago, when I didn't believe in Jesus, but was brought to a point of utter loneliness and desolation of spirit, almost suicidal. I knew then that I was desperately sick. But in due time, God brought me to Himself through the revelation of Jesus, His Son, so that I knew He was alive. My loneliness was healed when I read in His word, "I will never leave you nor forsake you" - *Hebrews 13:5*. What a wonderful promise, never to be truly lonely again, and the promise is eternal. You may not be able to name a day when He became your Friend, but perhaps gradually, you came to know and love Him. Such was His love that He died for us. What a Friend we have in Jesus, all our sins and grief to bear.

Jesus the Teacher

The people in our Lord's day were impressed not only by what He did, but by what He said, because He spoke as one having authority. He spoke with all the authority of one sent from God, but some of the things He said people found hard to accept. "This is a hard saying", they would complain. They were offended and some stopped following Him because of this. Jesus turned to His closest disciples and asked them, "Will you also go away?" "To whom shall we go?", they replied, "You have the words of eternal life." Even though they didn't fully understand, they recognised that one greater than Moses was here, and that no one had spoken as this man spoke, as one having authority.

Part of the sermon on the mount as recorded by Luke, contains what could be described as a hard saying. Jesus said, "Love your enemies, do good to those who hate you." Sometimes we may ask, why does God make demands on us we find impossible to carry out? Love your enemies! How can we love our enemies, when we sometimes find it difficult to love our friends? It is not humanly possible, being quite contrary to our fallen human nature. Our natural reaction is to hit back when we are hurt, to retaliate, to want to do harm to the person who has insulted or injured us. Revenge is what we seek in the name of justice. But our Lord says, "Love your enemies", not of course in a romantic sentimental sense, but in a practical sense, "Do good to those who hate you." It's to do with our actions, not with our feelings. We are to do good to our enemies even though our enemies might rebel at the very idea. But isn't that hypocrisy, doing good to someone we dislike intensely? Not at all. It is overcoming our feelings which may be entirely irrational, in obedience to our Lord's command. It is only by His love and power working in us that it becomes possible. As the Scripture says, "With men it is impossible, but with God, all things are possible." What is needed is an acknowledgement that we are at fault, falling short of God's perfect standards. We should not be content with that, but to actively desire to be what our Father wants us to be, and to co-operate with Him in bringing about the change. It is to hunger and thirst after righteousness, with the promise that we shall be filled.

Our Lord Jesus showed His love for His enemies supremely in His prayer from the cross for those who were tormenting and torturing Him to death, "Father, forgive them, they don't know what they are doing." In the midst of all the hate and pain, abandoned even by His closest friends, He could say that prayer. But we are easily offended by trivial things and annoyances. We may not think it too serious a thing to dislike somebody. We may call it personality clash, or ideological difference of opinion, or whatever euphemism we use. But it springs from the heart, which is "deceitful above all things". Where there is not love, there is hate, and where there is hate, there is murder. Listen to what the word of God says about this, "We know that we have passed from death to life, because we love the brethren. Anyone who does not love remains in death. Anyone who hates his brother is a murderer, and you know that no murderer has eternal life in him." - *John 3:14,15*. The stark reality of the fruits of hatred are revealed in tribal warfare, ethnic cleansing, barbaric maiming and killing on a massive scale. Christian witness is to forgive even such horror in response to our Lord's command. If there is no love in the Church, we have nothing to say to the world. Apart from loss of effective witness, perhaps the greatest incentive to love someone we personally dislike, or even find repulsive, is to recognise that this fellow human being is someone God loves, and for whom Jesus Christ died. Father, forgive us if we harbour any resentment or ill will against another person. Bring us to repentance, and by your Spirit fill us with love, compassion and forgiveness, to love our enemies, and do good to those who hate us. Amen.

Jesus the Teacher

78

Justice and Judgment

The two things for which the world cries out more than any other are, peace and justice. People long for peace, not only in the cessation of conflict between nations, but also within themselves. The world is full of injustice, where right and fairness are seen to be absent. The seemingly innocent suffer, and the oppressors appear to get away with their crimes. Christians see all this as a cosmic conflict between the forces of good and evil, between God the Creator, and Satan the fallen angel, intent on disharmony and destruction. The essential cause of conflict, violence and injustice lies within the human heart, described in the word of God as being "deceitful and desperately wicked". Where is true justice to be found, when human justice is so obviously flawed? So often the innocent suffer and the guilty go free, resulting in anger and frustration. Christians believe that there will be perfect justice in the final judgment, when Jesus Christ returns to the earth in glory at the end of time to judge the world. The word of God says that, "everyone of us must appear before the judgment seat of Christ", that is all people of all faiths and of none. We are all accountable and responsible to God for what we have done with the light we have received, and will be judged accordingly with perfect justice. There will be no miscarriage of justice on that day when the secrets of our hearts will be revealed, all hypocrisy and pretence done away. For those who have put their trust in Christ and Him alone for salvation, and whose lives bear witness to the presence of the Holy Spirit within, their faith will be tried and tested by fire to see how genuine it is. For many will say on that day, "Lord, Lord", but to some He will say, "I never knew you, depart from me."

Those who have refused to accept the free gift of salvation through faith in the shed blood of Christ for their redemption, will have to face judgment by the law of God which is a requirement of perfection in all thought, word and conduct. For some, perfect justice could be a fearful prospect where every aspect of a person's life, personality and environment will be fully taken into account, unlike human justice where only superficial evidence and circumstances can be examined and judgment reached. Salvation through faith in Jesus Christ means nothing unless it implies that some will knowingly and willingly reject it, and suffer the consequences.

References to hell in the Bible only come from the recorded words of Jesus Christ, and a warning to all who think that they can satisfy God's perfect standards by their own unaided efforts. There are some who will say, "God is love", and therefore He cannot possibly consign anyone, no matter how wicked, to eternal separation and punishment. If that is the case, then what is the meaning of salvation? What are we saved from, and what benefits do Christians derive from their faith? In other words, what does *John 3:16* mean when it says, "God loved the world so much that He gave His one and only Son, that whoever believes in Him should not perish, but have everlasting life"? Can Christians be smug about being 'the body of Christ', without thought and concern for those who do not claim to be part of that body? We talk about the gospel, the good news, but what do we mean by that, and why should we bother to spread it if nobody is going to be eternally lost?

Yes, God is love, and in His infinite love and mercy, has provided the way of salvation through the sacrificial death of His Son, our Lord and Saviour, Jesus Christ, for "there is no other name under heaven, given to humankind, whereby we must be saved." This free gift of God is conditional upon our acceptance of what is freely offered. We cannot escape having to give an account to God for all that we have said and done, but as forgiven sinners, we can escape the full requirements of the law because our Saviour, Christ, has paid the price and made full atonement for us, the "Lamb of God who takes away the sin of the world." - *John 1:29*

Just as it is certain that Christ will return to the earth in glory, so it is certain that He alone will judge the world in righteousness. The word of God declares it. The Church of Christ believes it. There is no other Judge, there is no other Saviour, there is no other Lord. When He comes we will bear the marks of crucifixion, because we died with Him. As the Apostle Paul says, "I have been crucified with Christ. It is no longer I who live, but Christ who lives in me, and the life I now live in the flesh, I live by faith in the Son of God who loved me, and gave Himself for me." - *Galatians 2:20*

Justification by Faith

It seems to me that we have two options in the religious life; to try to live according to the law of God, or to live by faith. The first is what most religions seek to do, to aspire to perfection in trying to please God by good works, sacrifice and meditation. In other words, by self effort. At first sight this seems to be a right and noble course. What else should we do if we want reward in this life, and in the life to come? The fundamental flaw in this is, that because of our innate sinful nature, it is impossible to achieve. It is whistling in the wind; a futile exercise. The law was brought in to show us the futility of trying to please God in this way, and to make us recognise our helplessness and our desperate need of a Saviour. In his letter to the Galatians, the Apostle Paul explains it like this - "All who rely on observing the law are under a curse, for it is written: cursed is everyone who does not continue to do everything written in the Book of the Law." That means everything, all the time, every day, every hour, every minute, every second. He goes on to say - "Clearly no one is justified by the law, because the righteous shall live by faith." And later he says - "Before this faith came, we were held prisoner by the law, locked up until faith should be revealed. So the law was put in charge to lead us to Christ that we might be justified by faith."

Martin Luther lived in Germany in the early 16th century, and was the first of the Protestant reformers. He was a Master of Arts, and later became a monk in the Order of Augustinian Friars. In this Order he was in bondage to strict observance of the law involving extreme acts of penance, self flagellation, walking on the knees, and such means of attempting to bring the flesh into subjection. He was delivered from this by reading the word of God in the

Apostle Paul's letter to the Romans when the truth of justification by faith and not by works, was revealed to him. His life was transformed by this, and he began to question some of the practices of the Church which were clearly in conflict with the word of God. One such practice was the selling of 'indulgences'. The current belief was that forgiven sin still had to be punished in this world or in purgatory. Indulgences from the Pope were said to cancel out the punishment, and they could be obtained by good works such as giving money to the Church. Naturally, Luther got into trouble with the Church over this and other doctrines, but refused to recant and was excommunicated. He could not go against his conscience and conviction. His final statement of defiance was – "Here I stand; I can do no other."

The Christian faith is unique among the all the world religions in that it starts from forgiveness and freedom, and doesn't work towards it. In His Son, Jesus Christ, God sets us free to serve Him in the world. The Gospel according to John makes it perfectly clear - "If the Son sets you free, you will be free indeed." What it amounts to is that unless we are free, and know that we are, we cannot be of much use to God to bring about His purposes in the world.   But in spite of all the assurances we find in the word of God that we are accepted and at one with Christ in His death and resurrection, there is often more than a sneaking suspicion that somehow we still have to earn salvation by good works, coming to church, taking communion, being kind and considerate to others. A picture of a God of Judgment marking all our failures down in His black book, is perhaps not very far from the back of our minds. But this is far from the truth and is a deception by the enemy of souls to keep us from recognising our true freedom in Christ. An important truth to keep in mind is contained in the Apostle Paul's letter to the Galatians when he says - "If righteousness could be gained by the law, Christ died for nothing." Think about that for a while if you are tempted to feel that it all depends on what we do and not what our Lord has already done. Maybe you are saying – "I don't need to know this. I know very well that I am free, not because I feel free, but because I believe what God has said in His word." This message is not for you, but there may be some who are not so sure, and are looking for reassurance. This is why it is so important to study the Bible and to know the wonderful promises God makes to His people.

Christians are the only people in the world who are truly free. Even those in the darkest, deepest prisons, compared with those who are without faith but with abundant wealth and physical freedom. Our freedom in Christ should be the means by which we can pass on our faith to those who are in bondage to fear, deceptions and superstitions. The message we are called to proclaim, the freedom of justification by faith, is summed up in this poem by Martin Luther:

I do not come because my soul is free from sin and pure and whole and worthy of Thy grace;
I do not speak to Thee because I've ever justly kept Thy laws and dare to meet Thy face.

I know that sin and guilt combine to reign o'er every thought of mine and turn from good to ill:
I know that when I try to be upright and just and true to Thee, I am a sinner still.

I know that often when I strive to keep a spark of love
alive for Thee, the powers within
leap up in un-submissive might and oft benumb
my sense of right and pull me back to sin.

I know that though in doing right I spend my life
I never could atone for all I've done;
but though my sins are black as night, I dare to come
before Thy sight because I trust Thy Son.

In Him alone my trust I place, come boldly to Thy
throne of grace and there, commune with Thee.
Salvation sure, O Lord is mine, and all unworthy
I am Thine, for Jesus died for me.

Light and Darkness

As an agnostic up to the age of about 30, I had no time or thought for Jesus Christ. But it was through the darkness of a very deep depression, desolation, intense loneliness, that I came to see the need of something outside of myself for deliverance. In the mercies of God, He brought me to a place where His Son Jesus, was revealed to me as a present living reality, and enabled me to make a commitment to that revelation. Light shone in the darkness! From that day on I was no longer agnostic, but a disciple of Jesus Christ. I was able to say with the Psalmist - "Before I was afflicted, I went astray; but now I keep your word." An inherent depressive tendency made me more dependent on God and less on myself. I discovered that God's power is made perfect in weakness. As He said to the Apostle Paul - "My grace is sufficient for you". What I have found is that healing is a continuous process of suffering and learning, until Christ returns to earth in power and glory at the end of the age. Light shines in the darkness, and the darkness has not overcome it.

Light and Darkness. These could be described as opposing forces, incompatible with each other, one trying to dominate the other. In a reading from the Gospel of John, Jesus said, "Walk while you have the light, so that darkness may not overtake you." If you walk in the darkness, you do not know where you are going. Three questions - What is the nature of light and darkness? Who or what is at the heart of the opposing forces of light and darkness? What is the role of the Church in this spiritual warfare?

What is the nature of light and darkness? Light is the natural phenomenon which makes things visible to us. It is also the symbol for what brings understanding to our minds. In a song of praise to God, the Psalmist says - "Your words give light; they give understanding to the simple." Light destroys darkness. When you go into a dark room and switch on the light, the darkness disappears. You can't switch on darkness. You can only switch off the light. Darkness is the absence of light. In the beginning of creation there was darkness, until God said - "Let there be light." In the Bible, light is the symbol for truth, love, holiness, goodness, hope, justice, peace, freedom, joy, kindness, victory, eternal life. Darkness is the symbol for lies, hate, evil, despair, slavery, misery, corruption, violence, death and destruction. Light can be as disturbing as darkness because it reveals not only beauty, but exposes imperfections, and in a spiritual sense, evil and sin.

Who or what is at the heart of the opposing forces of light and darkness? The Apostle John says that when our Lord Jesus Christ came into the world, He came as "the light that shines in the darkness." Jesus Himself says - "I have come into the world as light, so that no one who believes in me should stay in darkness." At His birth he faced forces that tried to destroy Him, in the person of King Herod. After His baptism in the Jordan, He was led into the desert to face the tempter, the devil, the personification of evil. He is described as the father of lies, the god of this world, who prowls around like a roaring lion seeking someone to destroy, but sometimes appears as "an angel of light." Jesus overcame lies with the authority and truth of the word of God, "it is written". The Apostle Paul says - "For our struggle is not against flesh and blood, but against the powers of this dark world, against the spiritual forces of evil in the heavenly realms." The reality of what we are up against is the evil forces which manifest themselves through human agents. People who are capable of making choices are faced with a clear choice, truth or lies, light or darkness. Jesus said: "This is the judgment, that the light has come into the world, but people loved darkness instead of light because their deeds were evil."

What is the role of the Church in this spiritual warfare? The Church is the Body of Christ. This means that we represent Christ on earth. His mission becomes our mission, as we respond to His great commission, to "go and make disciples." The word 'mission' is from the Latin meaning, 'sending'. Jesus said, "As the Father sent me, I am sending you." Our mission is summed up clearly in the mission to the Gentiles that Jesus gave to Saul of Tarsus on the road to Damascus, "I am sending you to them, to open their eyes and turn them from darkness to light, and from the power of Satan to God, so that they may receive forgiveness of sins and a place among those who are sanctified by faith in me." That, in essence, is the good news, the gospel we are called to proclaim in all we say and do. God's holiness is expressed in terms of light and the revelation of His love in Christ. This church is a lighthouse from which the light of the gospel of Christ must continue to shine out to souls at sea in our parish. It must shine as a beacon of hope into the darkness of ignorance, loneliness, superstition, despair, fear and hopelessness, with the light of the love of Christ. That is our mission, it's what we are here for. We are here to tell them that God loves them, that Jesus died for them, their sins are forgiven! All they need to do is to believe it and receive it. Light shines in the darkness, and the darkness has not overcome it.

Light of the World

The wise men from the East were drawn by the light of a star to the Light of the World, and when they found Him they worshipped him. The Light could not be hidden, but must be revealed, first to Mary and Joseph, then to the shepherds representing the pastoral care of the sheep of Israel, and finally to the foreigners, those who were far off, representing the Gentile world. An all encompassing revelation to immediate family, to the chosen people of Israel, and to the whole world. God's plan of redemption began with the calling and obedience of one man through whom all the nations of the world would be blessed. From the beginning God showed that this blessing would be based on faith, because Abraham believed God, and it was reckoned to him as righteousness; and he is the father of us all. Called out of slavery in Egypt, the nation of Israel under Moses was forged in the desert years, and brought into a land of their own which God had promised them. Through the prophets, God had promised deliverance from all their enemies; ultimately under the Kingship of the Anointed One, the Messiah who was to come. In due time God brought forth His Son, born of a virgin, in humble circumstances, as foretold by the prophet Isaiah. The tragedy for the Jews is that apart from a small collection of uneducated fishermen and others, they did not recognise Him when He came. The bad news is that His own people hounded Him to death. The good news is that through the death and resurrection of His Son, God has brought about the prospect of salvation for the whole world. Through Isaiah God says - "I will make you a light to the nations, to be my salvation to earth's farthest bounds." After Pentecost, the light of the gospel shone forth in the power of the Holy Spirit, in Jerusalem and Samaria and to the ends of the earth.

Over the centuries, men and women of vision, faith and courage, have taken the message of salvation to earth's farthest bounds. "The light shines in the darkness, and the darkness has not overcome it." We may be seeing a decline of faith in the western world, but there are parts of the world where the Church of Christ is on the move. In Africa, the Church is growing at a greater rate than the increase in population. The same is happening in parts of Asia. Atheistic Communism failed to extinguish the light of faith, and the collapse of that ideology has opened the floodgates for full expression of Christian worship. The China Inland Mission spread the gospel in that great country until, under Mao Tse Tung, it was expelled in 1952. The expelled missionaries went to other East Asian countries such as Malaya, Singapore, Borneo, Korea, Taiwan, Cambodia and Japan, as the Overseas Missionary Fellowship. A member of this church was a missionary with OMF working in Japan, and a small group was formed to pray for her work of church planting, creating a church where there was none. In teaching English to Japanese women, the gospel was preached. Some believed and were baptised, and so a church was formed. It was hard for these women to live out their faith in Christ in a culture based on ancestor worship, Shintoism and Buddhism. A light was lit in Japan, and nothing will put it out.

Missionaries are people of vision and prayer, and we must be the same if we are to be effective as witnesses in our own parish. The Church in England is no longer essentially pastoral, but a mission Church. The early Church devoted themselves to the Apostles' teaching, to the breaking of bread, and prayer. That was their priority, and it should be ours. We catch the vision of what God is calling us to do in the regular study of His word, through the teaching ministry of preaching and through prayer. It was through His knowledge of Scripture that our Lord Jesus recognised His appointed mission as Messiah. He knew at the age of twelve, and it was confirmed at His baptism in the River Jordan, when the Holy Spirit came upon Him, and His ministry began. Through prayer He aligned Himself with His Father's will, and became obedient unto death, even death on a cross.

God has a purpose for His Church here, but we will not catch the vision for it until we devote ourselves to teaching and prayer. It is essential for effective evangelism. Let us re-commit ourselves to Christ, and progress to regular Bible Study Groups or Prayer Cells, that we may become a centre for community and worship. Then others will be drawn to the light of our witness, and discover the Light of the World, and worship Him in the fellowship of His Church in this place. That Light cannot be hidden. Through the pain of fighting without and within, the Church will be purified, the gospel preached, and God's purposes fulfilled.

Light of the World

New Creation

If you want a description of what a Christian life should be like, I think there could be none better than the one from the Apostle Paul's letter to the church at Colossae - "Therefore as God's chosen people, holy and dearly loved, clothe yourselves with compassion, kindness, meekness, gentleness and patience. Forgive as the Lord forgave you. And over all these virtues put on love which binds them all together in perfect unity". You may think, well this is fine but an impossible standard for fallible human beings to achieve; and of course you would be right! But the letter is addressed to "God's chosen people, holy and dearly loved", and not to the world in general. It is addressed to people who by the indwelling of the Holy Spirit, should strive for such a standard and go someway to achieving it. Paul describes it in terms of clothing, like taking off old soiled clothes and putting on new clean ones, "seeing that you have stripped off the old self with its practices and have clothed yourselves with the new self, which is being renewed in knowledge according to the image of its Creator".

When we commit our lives to Jesus Christ, trusting in Him alone for salvation, and looking to Him to make us fit for eternity, nothing can ever be the same as it was. We become a new creation, outwardly the same, but inwardly completely changed. We have died to the old self and now, in union with Christ have been resurrected to a new self. We see ourselves for the first time as we really are in the sight of a holy God; and the things we might have thought of as acceptable, or excusable behaviour, are seen as old filthy rags. As soon as we see this we can't wait to get rid of them and put on the new spotless clothes of righteousness that we have received as a gift from our Lord and Saviour, Jesus

Christ. What it means is that we must live in the reality of what we are now in Christ, inseparable from Him, crucified with Him, risen with Him, ascended with Him, and hidden with Him in God. In writing to the Christians in Rome, the Apostle Paul says that we are to know ourselves as 'in Christ'; not that we are to struggle that somehow Christ may be in us.

The simple word 'therefore' often appears in Scripture as it does I my opening text. I like that word because it tells us that what is written follows as a direct result or consequence of what has gone before. So as we think about clothing ourselves with compassion, kindness, meekness, gentleness and patience, we must look back to what has gone before to see what makes this a logical conclusion. Earlier in his letter, Paul exhorts the church in Rome to - "Set your minds on things that are above, not on things that are on earth, for you have died, and your life is hidden with Christ in God". We have died to what we once were, and have become one with Christ, part of His body the Church. What He does, we do; where He goes, we go. So because we have this union and communion with Christ and are a new creation, we have a new standard of behaviour which is incompatible with what we once did. Therefore, off with the old and on with the new! By virtue of our union and communion with Christ, our past, present and future is covered. We have been justified (past); we are being sanctified (present); and shall be glorified (future). Justified means that we have been acquitted, declared righteous. Sanctified means that we are being made more like Jesus. Glorified means that we shall inherit all that Christ is, and will share in it eternally. When He comes again we hope for the perfection of our happiness. When He comes again there will be a meeting of all the saints, and those whose life is now hidden with Christ shall appear with Him in that glory which He Himself enjoys. "Therefore as God's chosen people, holy, and dearly loved, clothe yourselves with compassion, kindness, meekness, gentleness and patience. Forgive as the Lord forgave you. And over all these virtues put on love which binds them all together in perfect unity". Imagine what a difference that could make to our church, our community, our country and the world!

Promises, Promises

It is said that when doubt comes in the door, faith goes out the window. We cannot perhaps stop doubts coming in, but we do not have to entertain them, give them house room, make them feel at home. If they settle in and become established, they will be difficult to remove. Faith is the only effective doubt remover. But it must be based on facts, and not feelings, otherwise doubts will have a field day, and we shall find ourselves on a roller coaster ride.

We believe in the facts as recorded in Scripture, the truth of the gospel, and in a loving God who always keeps His promises. What He promises He will surely perform. It was through the prophet Isaiah that God foretold the promised Messiah, some eight hundred years before the birth of Jesus. Thousands upon thousands of faithful Jews would have been born and died without that promise having been fulfilled in their lifetime. Did they die disappointed, or in faith and hope that although they were not to see it, their children's children would? It was a long wait as we see it, but in God's own appointed time, the Virgin Mary gave birth to His Son, according to that which was spoken by the prophet - "The virgin will be with child, and will give birth to a son, and they will call him Immanuel which means, 'God with us'." At Christmas we look back to that time in history when God became man and dwelt among us. Then we look beyond Christmas and the baby lying in a manger, to a future time in history referred to by the Apostle Paul in his first letter to the Thessalonians, chapter 5 as - "The day of the Lord", also referred to frequently in Scripture, ominously, as "That day". It is what we call the second Advent when Christ will come again in glory to judge the living and the dead. About that day, Paul says, "About times and dates we do not need to write to you, for you know very well that the day of the Lord will come like a thief in the night." The early Christians lived in daily expectation of their Lord's return, but it did not happen. Now here we are two thousand years later, and still no second Advent. We are reminded every Sunday in the Eucharistic Prayer about the certainty of that event when we say, "Christ has died, Christ is risen, Christ will come again." This is our faith, our constant expectation, and we are encouraged to be ready, "As sons of the day, let us be alert and self-controlled." We do not know dates or times, but the day should not surprise us like a thief.

In the light of the knowledge of our salvation, and the certainty of our Lord's return, we are to encourage one another and build each other up, to be joyful always, pray continually, and give thanks in all circumstances. We have every reason to do so, but so very often we live in fear and uncertainty. We look forward to that day, but do we look forward to it in the sense of eager anticipation of that time when we will be with the Lord forever? Some things are worth waiting for, and whether we are awake or asleep, this will be the culmination of all our deepest longings, when we shall truly be made whole and enter into our inheritance in Christ. In that day, truth and justice and peace will prevail, and God will be all, and in all. In his second letter to the Corinthians, the Apostle Paul compares - "Our light and momentary troubles, with an eternal weight of glory that far outweighs them all." We should not walk through life with our heads in the clouds, unable to see what's going on around us, but neither should we be weighed down with burdens from which our Lord died to deliver us. We should live as sons and heirs, conscious of our true inheritance, not proud of our achievements, but knowing from what we have been delivered by the grace of God. Having been freed from anxiety about ourselves, we are free to turn our attention to the needs of others. Beginning with our families, friends, neighbours, and the people of our parish, who are in desperate need of the knowledge of the love of God in Jesus Christ.

In our witness for Christ we call upon the power of the Holy Spirit. Someone has said, "Real change begins when churches open their lives, doors, hearts, resources, time and energy to a local community." This is the work to which we have been called as we wait in eager anticipation for 'that day'. We travel hopefully with a living hope which does not disappoint us, because it is alive in our hearts by the Holy Spirit. The arrival will be far more glorious than we can possibly imagine. So let us encourage one another and build each other up. And to this end remember the very last words contained in the Revelation to John, chapter 22, verses 20 and 21, He who testifies to these things says, "Yes, I am coming soon." Amen. Come, Lord Jesus. The grace of the Lord Jesus be with God's people. Amen.

Repentance

John the Baptist was the last and greatest of the prophets, and lived in the desert of Judea, preaching a baptism of repentance for the remission of sins. His message was this: "Repent, for the kingdom of heaven is near." Baptism is a wonderful and joyful occasion. If Her Majesty the Queen was coming to Tyneside, nothing would be left to chance. Adequate preparations would be made to ensure that everything and everybody would be ready to receive her. Members of her staff would arrive well in advance to prepare the way for the sovereign. How much more was it necessary for the way to be prepared for the coming of the Son of God! John the Baptist was the one sent by God for this purpose, to tell the people of Israel that their long awaited Messiah would soon be here, and to prepare themselves to receive Him. They were not to build a palace or prepare a banquet for their King, but to turn from their evil ways, confess their wrongdoings, and so be ready to recognise Him and follow Him when He appeared. People recognised John as a prophet, and some thought that he could even be the Messiah himself. But John knew that he was the one spoken about by the prophet Isaiah - "A voice of one calling in the desert. Prepare the way of the Lord, make straight paths for Him." The people responded to his message, went out to him confessing their sins, and were baptized by him in the River Jordan.

What exactly is repentance, why was it necessary, and why were people baptized? Repentance in the Old Testament means turning away from sin to God, and in the New Testament refers to a change of mind, a radical transformation of thought, outlook and direction. The Apostle Paul says - "Godly sorrow brings repentance that leads to salvation." As sin is at the heart of our problem in relation to God, the salvation to which repentance is directed is salvation from sin. There can be no salvation without repentance, which is why John came first preparing the way, preaching the baptism of repentance. The famous evangelist, Billy Graham, has always stressed the need for repentance in his preaching; a turning away from all we know to be wrong, and a willingness to turn to God. A recognition that we are heading in the wrong direction, and turning round to face the other way is a necessary step to finding the path that leads to life in all its fullness. Baptism was the means by which the people visibly and publicly, declared their need for forgiveness, by immersion in the River Jordan. In effect they were agreeing with what God was saying through His prophet, and wanted to do something about it. There were some who did not agree; sadly, some of the religious leaders of the day who came out of curiosity to see what was going on, and did not feel the need to repent. John had some harsh words to say to them.

Baptism today is not a baptism of repentance as preached by John, although that is part of it. Rather it is based on what the Apostle Peter said to the people on the Day of Pentecost when the Holy Spirit came in great power on the assembled disciples. He said this - "Repent and be baptized every one of you in the name of Jesus Christ for the forgiveness of your sins." In infant baptism, obviously small babies cannot repent, and have as yet done nothing wrong, but the questions are asked of those acting on their behalf; parents and godparents. "Do you turn to Christ? Do you repent of your sins? Do you renounce evil?" The essential sequence is repent and be baptised. Baptism is the symbolic cleansing by washing, and in baptism by immersion, is symbolic of dying to the old life, and rising again to the new life in Christ. The service of Baptism begins by the minister saying - "Children who are too young to profess the Christian faith are baptized on the understanding that they are brought up as Christians within the family of the Church." That puts the responsibility on those who, on the basis of their own declared faith, must ensure that as far as they are able, by their teaching and example, that children can make real for themselves the promises made on their behalf. No matter what advantages or disadvantages we have, we are all ultimately responsible to God for our own actions. Everything will be measured against our personal response to God's love for us as revealed in His Son, Jesus.

A new life is an exciting event with all its hopes and possibilities. Elizabeth and Zechariah, the parents of John the Baptist, had high expectations for their son, but he had to be brought up in the real world with all its dangers and hardships. We look at the world today and have reason to be fearful for the future of our children; the sort of culture and influences which will affect their lives.   There is a power of lawlessness against which Christians are called to fight. The rebellion against authority we see today is in essence a reflection of our rebellion against the authority of God. In our own country, and in the western world generally, there has been a turning away from God and His righteous ways. The Scripture says in Proverbs 14 verse 34 - "Righteousness exalts a nation, but sin is a disgrace to any people.". Nothing short of national repentance is required, a turning around, recognising that we are heading the wrong way. If we are looking at political solutions, various philosophies, or wealth and prosperity to solve our problems, we are looking in the wrong direction, because our sickness is spiritual, and one that only God in Jesus Christ can heal. The good news for us, and for the whole world, is that God has done everything for us through His Son, the one for whom John the Baptist came to prepare the way. God was in Christ reconciling the world to Himself.   Christians don't like to talk about repentance and judgment. We would much prefer to talk about the love and forgiveness of God. It is interesting to note that in the Acts of the Apostles which records the birth of the Church and its powerful witness, the word 'love' does not occur at all, but the word 'repent' occurs several times.   The message today, for renewal in the Church and revival for all who have turned away from God, echoes the message of John the Baptist, and words to be found in the service of Baptism - "Repent of your sins. Renounce evil. Turn to Christ."

Rights and Responsibility

It seems to me that one of the fundamental ills besetting present day society is an imbalance between rights and responsibility, with the scales heavily loaded in favour of rights. My rights; your responsibility. A classic case springs to mind about a schoolboy who was so disruptive in class that his teachers refused to teach him. His parents claimed their rights under the law for their son to be taught in school, in spite of his unruly behaviour, which nearly resulted in a teachers' strike. A compromise was reached, but it is clear that the parents accepted no responsibility for their son's actions. Time was when a child could have expected equal treatment at home if he had been disciplined at school.

There are human rights to be fought for at all costs, and thousands have died resisting an oppressor seeking to deny basic freedoms. But this is sacrificial with the intention of preserving or gaining rights for other people, at considerable cost to the individual. Selfish pre-occupation with our own rights is the basic cause of conflict. We see it in disputes between neighbours over boundaries or hedges. Domestic warfare. In the letter to the Philippians chapter 2, the Apostle Paul exhorts us to - "Do nothing out of selfish ambition or vain conceit, but in humility consider others better than yourselves. Each of you should look not only to your own interests, but also to the interests of others." Sinful human nature cannot achieve this on a long term, consistent basis, even though attempts may be made at this ideal. It can spring only from being united with Christ, and fellowship with the Holy Spirit, and then only as we yield ourselves more and more to His control. Our aim should not be our rights, but our righteousness, as we seek to be conformed to the image of the blessed Son of God.

God has rights. In fact, He has every right, but in His infinite love and forbearance, chooses not to claim them; at least not by force. His way is love and gentle persuasion.

He seeks those who are wiling and available to Him as they respond to His love for them.   We are to look to the example of our Lord and Saviour, "Who being in very nature God, did not consider equality with God something to be grasped, but made Himself nothing, taking the very nature of a servant, being made in human likeness." He, above all, could have claimed His rights. At the time of His arrest in Gethsemane, He could have called more than twelve legions of angels to His aid; a force mightier than any ever seen on earth, just waiting for the word. Then why did He not? "But how then would the Scriptures be fulfilled which say it must happen this way?" *Matthew 26:54.*   He did not claim His rights, but "humbled Himself, and became obedient to death, even death on a cross." *Philippians 2:8.*   In so doing, He took upon Himself the responsibility for our sins, the sins of the whole world. In taking up the cross He literally shouldered the blame. What a contrast to the general attitude of natural man! Passing the buck is the name of the game. We see this clearly in politics, where no one can be seen to be taking the blame when things go wrong. It's the fault of someone else, the opposition, or 'what we inherited'. A scapegoat must be found or our job is at risk, or worse still, we won't be re-elected. It's difficult to be honest in politics. Genuine humility is in short supply.

How should we behave as a Church in the light of all this? We are to live in love, humility and service to one another, because we are a family of persons who share a common life in Christ. Not a collection of individuals who happen to meet in church every Sunday. Our attitude should be the same as that of our Lord Jesus, who did not aggressively exploit the power, but revealed the true nature of being God in self-giving love. There is no room in the Church for grasping hold of our own particular churchmanship at all costs, and hating or despising what other people are doing in their service for Christ. The world looks for love and truth, and often only sees hypocrisy. On the cross our Lord emptied Himself and poured Himself out completely for the whole world, holding nothing back. But we grasp tenaciously what we have, our ministry, our traditions, our reputation, our churchmanship; drawing them up around us until they become an impenetrable wall of defence, fearful lest they are stripped away and we are found naked. He was naked on the cross, no dignity, no defence, no rights, helpless, despised, abused, rejected by everyone. Crucifixes sanitize the image, but the reality was that He hardly resembled a human being. As the prophet Isaiah says - "There were many who were appalled at Him; His appearance was was so disfigured beyond that of any man, and His form marred beyond human likeness." - *Isaiah 52:14.* This is what He willingly chose, agreed to endure, the Lord of all creation! This was the end product of His ministry. Complete and utter failure in the eyes of the world, but to the Father, and those who believe, the greatest victory of all time! And so we come to the ultimate triumph as proclaimed by the Apostle Paul in his letter to the Philippians - "Therefore God exalted Him to the highest place, and gave Him the name that is above every name, that at the name of Jesus every knee should bow, in heaven and on earth and under the earth, and every tongue confess that Jesus Christ is Lord, to the glory of God the Father." On that day, those who judged Him will themselves be judged, and the scales of rights and responsibility will be perfectly balanced.

Seeds, Storms, and Satan

Seeds

The sower and the seed and the farmer. In the work of grace there must be a sower. The natural earth is the mother of weeds, and must be ploughed and planted to produce fruit. The heart of humankind is like the barren earth, dead towards God. It needs the seed of God's word and grace to make it grow and mature. Farmers cannot explain how the seed in the ground develops. All they know is to plant seeds and wait for the harvest. They leave the growth to God. We cannot explain how grace works in the heart; how in some it produces fruit, and in others none. God alone can give life to the lifeless, and our principal work is to sow the seed. Life manifests itself gradually. A plant goes through many stages, but at every stage it is a living thing, but there is no harvest until the plant is ripe. How slowly it grows to produce the harvest of abundance and fruitfulness.

The kingdom of God is like a grain of mustard seed. It is a parable of the growth of the Church of Christ from very small beginnings. For Jews the mustard seed was an expression of something small and insignificant. Such was the beginning of the Church of Jesus Christ with a small group of unlearned disciples. Once planted at Pentecost, the Church has grown into a worldwide religion, and is still growing rapidly. The mission of the Church is to make disciples, to be fruitful and multiply. The whole earth shall be filled with the glory of God. Nothing can stop it. The little seed becomes a great tree.

Storms

Few events contain more rich instruction than the storm on the Sea of Galilee. Christ's service does not exempt His servants from storms, afflictions. The faithful disciples were in danger of being drowned. Experienced fishermen were terrified for their lives. We have wonderful promises from God, but He has never promised that we shall have no afflictions. Through them, He draws us closer to Himself, exposes our weaknesses. "It is good for me that I have been afflicted." Our Lord Jesus was truly man. In the storm He was asleep in the ship. He had a body just like ours in all respects. He is as truly man as He is truly God. He knows all our infirmities, afflictions, weaknesses. He has experienced them all in His own body. He experienced hunger, pain, every emotion and temptation. So we can learn to trust Him completely in whatever happens in our lives. We were created for a purpose, and He is in complete control. Our Lord Jesus Christ has almighty power. He speaks to the wind and the waves and they obey Him. The words of Him through whom all things were made – "Peace be still." Elements and creatures obey Him at His command. He can still the storms that arise in our lives as we appeal to Him for calm. Even when we face death, we are in the ship with Christ. He is exceedingly patient with our lack of faith. He dealt tenderly with His disciples in their fear – "Where is your faith?" Let us take comfort that we believe and trust in Christ, even though we err in many ways. God sees His Son in us as we submit to His will and authority. So, we are able to stay calm in all circumstances, and this is a witness to the troubled world.

Satan

Demonic possession was a real and true thing in the time of our Lord's earthly ministry. This is distinct from human sickness and disease, but we try to rationalize, to reason it out. Many do not accept the existence of a powerful spiritual enemy; Satan and his host of demons. Satan is an extremely cruel, powerful and malicious being. His purpose is to destroy and corrupt. He is described by Jesus as "the god of this world, a liar and the father of lies."

Our Lord has complete power and authority over the devil. Demons can do nothing without His permission. Our powerful enemy is defeated, but still active until the final triumph when Christ returns in power and glory at the end of the age. His work of healing continues in our hearts and minds as we watch and pray, and look to Him for all our needs. Jesus delivered a demon possessed man from the power of Satan, and he wanted to follow Christ as His disciple. But Jesus had different plans for him, which was to stay home and witness to his family and friends' Our conduct after conversion may be full of errors as we adapt to a new way of life. God's plan for us may be quite different from what we expect. Have we nothing to tell others? A believer's own family have first claim on his attention. If we have not been born again we have nothing to say. God knows very well how we will react after conversion. This does not stop Him from choosing us as witnesses to the gospel in spite of our weakness. We are not to be discouraged by any failure. Nothing is wasted when He chooses to appoint us for service. In everything He works for our good and for the benefit of others.

Sheep and Shepherds

Did you know that we are all like sheep? References to sheep and shepherds occurs often in both the Old and New Testaments. God calls His people, "my sheep". The shepherds are the rulers of Israel, and God Himself is often called the Shepherd of His people. "He led forth His people like sheep, and guided them in the desert like a flock, and He brought them to His holy land." - *Psalm 78:52*. Sheep and shepherds give us a wonderful picture of the relationship between God and His people. The idea of our likeness to sheep is not a flattering one. Sheep are timid, helpless and rather stupid creatures, prey to every kind of danger without someone to care for them and protect them. The shepherd was a familiar figure in Palestine. He spent much of his life with his flock, and his own sheep knew and responded to his voice. He led (not drove) them to fresh grazing, and guarded them from wild animals by lying across the entrance to the sheepfold at night, so becoming its 'door'. David was the shepherd king. His fearless defence of his flock against lions and bears, gave him the courage he would need to go against Goliath in the name of the Lord of Hosts, and prepared him for kingship. So he was able to compose that most beautiful and greatly loved of psalms that we know as the 23rd Psalm. "The Lord is my shepherd I shall not want. He makes me lie down in green pastures, he leads me beside still waters, he restores my soul." The graphic and poetic language speaks of peace and tranquillity even in the face of death, evil and enemies, the promise of goodness, mercy and eternal life. It is balm to the soul, and has, and still does, bring comfort to people in distress, even to those who do not know the true Shepherd.

The story of the lost sheep in the Gospel of Luke chapter 15, shows the infinite worth of an individual life in the sight of God. One sheep will look very much like another to us, and there are thousands of them in Northumberland. But the shepherds know each one, and if one is lost they will go to great lengths to find it. We may feel very insignificant as individuals, and perhaps even worthless, but to God we are very precious. So great is His love, that He can relate to each one of us as if we were the only person in the world that matters to Him. That is exciting and humbling. Jesus came to seek and to save that which was lost. He knows each one of us intimately, and looks for a response of love, as He reveals Himself to us in personal ways to which only we can respond. Just as a shepherd calls his sheep, so He calls us by name.

Our Lord had compassion on the people of His day, because He saw them as, "Harassed and helpless like sheep without a shepherd." - *Matthew 9:36*. Do we see those who do not know Christ, as sheep without a shepherd? Surely it should be our heart's desire that they should know Him as their Shepherd? We live under the eternal protection of the shepherd and guardian of our souls. To live outside of that protection is to be lost, and prey to every lie and deceit of the enemy of souls. Our Lord will not be satisfied until He has brought every lost sheep into the safety of the fold. He calls us to share in the work so that there will be one flock, one shepherd. As He said to His disciples, so He says to us, "I am sending you out as sheep among wolves." - *Matthew 10:16.* Both command and compassion send us out into a dangerous world, and we go as helpless in ourselves, but confident in the love, guidance and protection of our Lord Jesus.

Those who exercise authority and control over others, are responsible to God for how they perform that task. A minister of the Church is called to exercise pastoral care over those in his or her charge. In the early Church, elders were appointed to take spiritual charge of the infant churches. So today, some church leaders are called 'pastors' from the Latin 'pascere', meaning 'to feed'. Our Lord gave this charge to the Apostle Peter, "Feed my sheep", a responsibility for which he would be answerable to God. He had harsh words to say to the shepherds or rulers of Israel, through the prophet Ezekiel. They had fed themselves, and had not cared for the people. "Thus says the Lord God, I am against the shepherds, and I will require my sheep at their hand."- *Ezekiel 34:10*. This brings home the responsibility of those who are called to be leaders in the Church. It is both a privilege, and an awesome calling.

Sheep are valuable, but also expendable, available to people as food, clothing and sacrifice. They offer no resistance to human treatment. In His dealings with humankind through His people Israel, God decreed that sheep should be offered up as a sacrifice for sin. It is a picture of the offering up of the innocent for the guilty, which becomes supremely relevant in the offering up of the Lamb of God; "the just for the unjust, that He might bring us to God." - *1 Peter 3:18*. It is an amazing thought that our Lord Jesus is both the "great Shepherd of the sheep", and the sacrificial Lamb that takes away the sin of the world. "Like a lamb that is led to the slaughter, and like a sheep before its shearers is dumb, so He opened not His mouth. Yet it was the will of the Lord to bruise Him, He has put Him to grief when He makes Himself an offering for sin." - *Isaiah 53:7*

Sheep and Shepherds

Signs of Glory

Have you ever stood in front of one of those distorting mirrors at a fair, or at the end of a seaside pier, and experienced a mixture of horror and amusement at the reflection you see; a grotesque distorted image, short and fat, tall and thin? We laugh at what we see because we know it is not a true reflection of what we really look like.   Imagine how we would feel if we were stuck with our distorted image. The Book Genesis tells us that we were created in the image of God, that is, we reflected in some way what God is like; not perhaps our physical appearance, but our nature, our capacity to be creative, to love, to communicate, to laugh, enjoy beauty. But we learn that sin came in and spoiled the relationship with our Creator, and distorted His image within us. Our nature became so corrupted by disobedience and rebellion, that we became outcast from the presence of God. In our fallen state we were no longer a true reflection of our Creator, and as sons of Adam, we all inherit the defective spiritual gene called sin.   We have all sinned and fall short of the glory of God. We read a lot about glory in the Scriptures, but how can we define it? No one can say exactly what it means. In relation to God it has to do with His reputation, the revelation of His being, of His very nature. It is all that is worthy of honour and praise, the splendour and beauty of creation, the beauty and bliss of heaven in the eternal presence of the Creator. The glory of Yahweh was shown in the cloud which led the people of Israel through the desert. The cloud rested on Mount Sinai where Moses saw His glory. No one could see God's face and live, but some vision of His glory was granted. But supremely it is revealed in the person and work of God's Son, our Lord Jesus Christ. As the writer of Hebrews says, "He reflects the glory of God and bears the very stamp of His nature, upholding the universe by His word of power." The glory of God was seen by the shepherds at the birth of Jesus, by His disciples throughout His incarnate life, and the signs that He did, things which only God could do. The first of these signs was at the wedding at Cana in Galilee when He changed water into wine. The Apostle John tells us that He thus revealed His glory and His disciples put their faith in Him.

The authority of His teaching, and other miraculous signs, the healings, raising the dead to life, and above all His own sacrificial death, resurrection and ascension, were all manifestations of the glory of God. The Pharisee Nicodemus said, "No one could do the signs that you do unless God was with him." And yet the Jewish leaders were so blinded by jealousy and hate that they refused to acknowledge the clear evidence that was being presented to them. Their minds and hearts were so poisoned that they accused Him of being possessed by demons. White was black to them, and you can't get further away from God than that. It is blasphemy against the Holy Spirit from which there is no road back. But we are of the household of faith, and we look for His coming in glory at the end of the age. On a specific date and time, Jesus was born of the Virgin Mary. On a specific date and time, He was baptized in the River Jordan. On specific dates and times, He was crucified, rose again from the dead and ascended into heaven. As we look for His return in glory, we can expect this too to be a specific date and time in history. Only the Father knows when that will be. Our Lord Himself prophesied the signs of the end of the age as recorded by Matthew, "At that time, the sign of the Son of Man will appear in the sky, and all the nations of the earth will mourn. They will see the Son of Man coming on the clouds of the sky, with power and great glory." The sign that will appear in the sky is open to speculation. My own personal view is that the sign will be one that everyone will recognize and identify with Christ, the sign of the cross. We look to 'that day' with eager anticipation, because He is coming to take us to be with Him in glory forever. That is the inheritance of those who have put their trust in Jesus Christ and His finished work on the cross.

Until 'that day' there is work for us to do. The object of the Church is to see that the world acknowledges the glory which is God's and turns to Him in repentance and faith. It is only the Church, imperfect as it is, that can reflect something of God's glory. God sees us in His Son, no longer in the distorting mirror of sin. We are in effect Christ to the world, and their view of the nature of God will largely depend on what they see in us. Distorted human nature gives a distorted picture of what God is like. Yet it is in that very distortion that God comes to us through His Son to heal and restore. An imperfect world, to some people, indicates an imperfect God, if indeed He exists to them at all. The whole of creation declares the glory of God. Jesus Christ and His Church declare the glory of God. People will see it through the love of Jesus reflected in our eyes, in our compassion, our willingness to suffer with them, and rejoice with them. That is how it will be until He comes again in the clouds of heaven. Then, every knee will bow and confess that Jesus Christ is Lord, to the glory of God the Father. The distorting mirror of sin will be finally put away, and everything restored to how God intended it to be in His perfect kingdom.

Spiritual Power

The keyword today is 'power', and in particular the power of the Holy Spirit; that power which came upon the disciples at Pentecost, and transformed them into bold preachers of the gospel. The word power is defined as control, dominion or authority, military force or potential, and a particular form of energy, such as nuclear power. One of the Greek words for power in the New Testament is 'dunamis', from which we derive 'dynamite' and 'dynamic'. Some of the hymns we sing are in fact prayers asking, pleading, for the power of the Holy Spirit. Hymns such as, "Come down O love divine"; "O breath of life come sweeping through us"; "Spirit of the living God fall afresh on us." Wonderful, inspiring words. But do we really want that power to transform our lives? There are three aspects of the work of the Holy Spirit which I want to draw to your attention; the Holy Spirit with us; within us, and upon us. Our Lord told His disciples that, "He dwells with you, and will be in you." The Holy Spirit is with us, and generally in the world, working to bring people to faith in Jesus Christ. As we respond and commit ourselves in faith, we have the Spirit within, the seal or guarantee that we truly belong to Christ.

Our confession from the heart that "Jesus is Lord", is the evidence of the Holy Spirit within. The very last words of our Lord to His disciples was the promise that they would be baptized with the Holy Spirit, "You will receive power when the Holy Spirit comes upon you; and you will be my witnesses." The disciples had received the Spirit within them in that upper room after the resurrection, but now the power came upon them in such a dramatic way at Pentecost. We read in *Acts 2:33* - "Therefore being by the right hand of God exalted, having received of the Father the promise of the Holy

Spirit, He has shed forth this which you now see and hear." The Lord Jesus is exalted, therefore the power of the Holy Spirit has been poured out, the evidence that Jesus is at the right hand of the Father, that He is in fact, Lord. The Spirit is with us to bring us to repentance and faith; within us to guarantee us life; and upon us to give us power for service and ministry.   The first two refer to the person of the Holy Spirit, and the last to the impersonal power that He imparts. At the River Jordan the power of the Holy Spirit came upon Jesus and His ministry began. At Pentecost the power was poured out and the Church was born.

Some may say, that's all very well; that power was needed at that time to lift the rocket ship, the Church, off the ground and into orbit. It doesn't happen now. Many will be familiar with the testimony of John Wesley when, on one occasion, he felt his heart strangely warmed, and an assurance was given to him that Christ had taken away his sins, and he did trust in him alone for salvation. This was the Spirit within. About six months later in the company of about sixty at a prayer meeting, he says, "About three in the morning the power of God came mightily upon us, inasmuch as many cried out for exceeding joy, and many fell to the ground. And they broke out with one voice, 'we praise thee O God; we acknowledge thee to be the Lord."   It was in that power that John Wesley preached the gospel up and down the land, and thousands were converted to faith in Jesus Christ.

The analogy of the power station may be helpful to illustrate the work of the Spirit upon the Church. Power or energy is produced by fire, wind and water, all symbols of the

Holy Spirit. Electric current cannot be seen as it passes through the cables, but without it everything would grind to a halt. Just think of the chaos that ensues during a power cut. Our demand for power is satisfied as we switch on at our consumer unit, and the energy flows for whatever purpose we have for it. The power grid can be overloaded, but the power of the Holy Spirit is without limit. It is that power by which the universe was created, and by which our Lord was raised from the dead. It is available to us by the flick of a switch which is our faith. If we are satisfied and content with the way we are, then we will have closed the door to the power of the Holy Spirit, and all that He seeks to do in and through us.   Status quo satisfaction leaves our Lord outside the door knocking to come in, just as with the church at Laodicea - *Revelation 3:14 to 22.* Are we prepared to have Christ standing among us in His risen power to reign as Lord, or do we want to retain control? Openness is the key to receiving the power of the Holy Spirit. Our Lord said, "If you being evil, know how to give good gifts to your children, how much more will the heavenly Father give the Holy Spirit to those who ask Him."   Ask, and it will be given to you, but ask in faith, which is the key to receiving all God's promises. There are no stereotypes in receiving power; the wind blows where it wills, but fundamental to it is recognition of need, awareness of our own impotence in the spiritual battle.

Temptation

Temptation! What is temptation? Well, everyone knows what temptation is. It is wanting to do something we know we shouldn't do, or to have something we know we shouldn't have. It is to do with the delight of the eye, the inward desire and enticement from without. Go on, do it, have it, what harm will it do? You deserve it, you need it, you'll be less of a person without it. Reason argues with conscience, and faith is needed to settle the contest. The other extreme is to run away from everything that looks good or feels good, in the belief that therefore it must be bad for us.

For Christians, the word temptation has more sinister, more spiritual connotations, and has to do with choices that may affect our relationship with God. It cannot affect our eternal destiny, but at least our reward in heaven. In our Scripture readings we see how our first parents dealt with temptation, or rather failed to deal with it, and how our Lord Jesus Christ dealt with it. We see that there was a third party involved, a malevolent being whose purpose is to draw us away from God's will and bring us into bondage to lies. We are deceived if we do not recognise the reality that lies behind the evil in the world. But we have at our disposal all the spiritual resources we need to overcome temptation. What are the truths concerning temptation which Scripture has to show us, and which we need to be aware of if we are to grow to maturity in Jesus Christ? The Biblical idea of temptation is not primarily of seduction, but of making trial of a person for the benevolent purpose of proving or improving quality, as well as the malicious aim of showing up weaknesses or trapping into wrong action.

Let's look at three aspects of this testing as it applies to us. First, people testing God; second, God testing His people; and third, Satan testing God's people.   We can test God by challenging Him to prove the truth of His words, and the goodness and justice of His ways. We do this, for example when we consider some disaster that has occurred in our own, or in other people's lives, and suggest that God is not in control, or that He doesn't really care. The danger in that is that we may turn away from God altogether in bitterness and disbelief. This was the attitude of the people of Israel when they complained to Moses in the desert, and even wished that they had died in captivity in Egypt. God tests His people by putting them in situations which reveal the quality of their faith and devotion. This testing in Scripture is likened to refining precious metal. Through the prophet Zechariah, God says - "I will refine them as one refines silver, and test them a gold is tested." And through the prophet Isaiah, He says - "Behold, I have refined you.........I have tried you in the furnace of affliction." All this is positive and is intended to purify and strengthen, not to break down, and destroy. The Apostle Peter's faith and devotion was challenged and tested in this way, when three times he was challenged to confess his allegiance to his Lord. The poverty of his self-reliance was revealed, and he wept bitterly when he recognised it.   Satan tests God's people by manipulating circumstances within the limits God allows him, in an attempt to make them desert God's will. Christians are the special object of the devil's attentions in trying to make them fall, and we must be constantly watchful and active in resisting him. He may try to crush us under the weight of hardship or pain, as in the story of Job, or urge us to wrong fulfilment of natural desires, making us careless, or by misrepresenting God. From the beginning, Satan, in the guise of the serpent, sought and succeeded in bringing humankind into the bondage of lies. First he planted the seed of doubt, and then flatly contradicted what God had said. The woman was tempted by the appearance of the fruit of the tree, and believed the lie. So did the man, and they both fell from grace. In our Lord's temptation in the desert He shows us the way to deal with it. In each attempt to turn Him aside from God's will, Jesus counters the lie with the truth of Scripture, the written word of God, even when the devil misapplies Scripture for his own ends. "It is written", says Jesus. The word of God is truth and can be relied upon in any situation. To weaken or diminish it, and cast doubt on its authority is to play into, the hands of the devil. The first question he posed to our first parents was - "Did God say?" And he is still doing it.

What then can we learn from all this for our comfort, support and encouragement? Although it is true that we have a powerful spiritual enemy, his power is limited by God, and his days are numbered. Temptation itself is not sin. It only becomes sin when we surrender to it, and in effect agree with it. Our Lord Jesus Christ was tempted in all points as we are, yet without sin. As the writer of Hebrews puts it - "Since He Himself passed through the test of suffering, He is able to help those who are meeting their test now." He will not allow us to be tested beyond our endurance, but with the test will provide a way of escape that we may be able to bear it. Our knowledge and understanding of God's word will enable us to counter lies with the truth. He will never leave us nor forsake us. Nothing is able to separate us from the love of Christ. In all our trials and temptations, we can truly say - "Thanks be to God who gives us the victory through our Lord Jesus Christ."   "It is written."

The Breath of God

"Breathe on me breath of God, fill me with life anew." The breath of God is the Holy Spirit who gives life to the Church, and without whom we would be a bag of bones, dry and lifeless, just like those in the valley described by the prophet Ezekiel. The Holy Spirit can be as gentle as breath and as powerful as the wind, as on the day of Pentecost. He is spoken of in the powerful symbols of wind, fire and water, all elements used in the generation of power. His is the power that creates, heals, raises from the dead, empowers the Church, makes us more like Jesus, and bestows gifts for service. We need to acknowledge that without Him we can do nothing. He produces in us the fruit described in *Galatians 5:22* - "The fruit of the Spirit is love, joy, peace, patience, kindness, goodness, faithfulness, gentleness, self control. Contrast this with the works of the flesh described in the previous verses, the horror that produces the things we read about in the media every day. The Apostle Paul likens the Church to a single body with its many limbs and organs. We say - "We are the body of Christ. In the one Spirit we were all baptized into one body." The analogy of the body is important for us to understand, because when we do, we will be more likely to live and work together in love and harmony. There are too many divisions in the Church because we do not understand diversity. Suspicion can lead to separation, and separation can lead to hate, and hate can lead to death. That is why Jesus gave us the command to love one another. The law is summed up in that one word and it is the first mentioned in those attributes described as the fruit of the Spirit.

The Apostle Paul told the church at Corinth that he did not want them to be ignorant about spiritual gifts. He explained what the gifts are and how they are to be used in the Church for the benefit of all, for the proper working of the body of Christ. He says to each one the manifestation of the Spirit is given for the common good. A gift is not perfected until it is willingly received and used. As Paul himself says - "Eagerly desire the greater gifts." Would we put a gift into the hands of our children of which they were not able and willing to make use? Jesus said - "If you being evil know how to give good gifts to your children, how much more will the Father give the Holy Spirit to those who ask Him." Whatever we lack we can ask for in faith, and we need to recognise the gifts in ourselves and in others. The gifts are generally recognised in the tasks we are called upon to do. Helping others, teaching, and administration are obvious ones, but where are the prophets, the workers of miracles, those with gifts of healing? Do these no longer apply? Are they no longer available? Or is it that we lack the faith to receive and use them? We need to ask the question concerning things which are clearly taught in Scripture as applying to the Church and which appear to be so necessary in the full and proper working of the body of Christ and its witness to the world. Everyone knows that there is no such thing as a perfect church. But we should aim at it, make it our goal, even though we fail.

Certainly we need spiritual gifts and to display the fruit of the Spirit. The vision of what God is able to do in a church cannot belong to a few who are determined to see it through at all costs. Perhaps it must start with a few consciously seeking the mind of Christ and sharing that with as many as are open to it. In the end it must be a common vision. There must be a consensus otherwise little or no progress can be made. It won't emerge in tablets of stone or be seen in writing on the wall, but will evolve as we pray together, study God's word, and co-operate in love, not looking inward but outward to a world desperately in need of Jesus Christ and His love. Some may say why not leave things as they are? It is because the Church is dynamic, not a static body. We pray for the Holy Spirit to come sweeping through us, to bend and break us till we humbly confess our need.   It is not a comfortable notion, but one which involves change and pain. It has ever been so. We talk about a wind of change, and that is what the Holy Spirit brings. If we put up barriers, close the doors and windows, we become stagnant, a bag of bones, a museum, with our Lord not in our midst, but outside the door knocking to come in to His Church. Let us then, open the doors of our hearts and minds without fear, looking unto Jesus the author and finisher of our faith. As we do this, the Holy Spirit will produce in us the fruit of love, joy and peace, and bestow the spiritual gifts we need.

"We are the body of Christ. In the one Spirit we were all baptized into one body. Let us then pursue all that makes for peace and builds up our common life." Amen

The Creation

I think that there are very few people who have not at some point been overcome with awe and wonder at the beauty of Creation. A particular combination of circumstances coupled with, perhaps, a beautiful sunrise or sunset over the sea or landscape, can produce an intense emotional response which is deep and satisfying. Or it may be the sight and scent of a single flower which has the same effect. For most people in the UK, the Lake District is particularly beautiful and awe inspiring. Clear blue skies and autumn colours sometimes reflect in the lakes like a tapestry. That, combined with the awesome fells, can seem like the nearest thing to heaven on earth. No wonder poets lived in the Lake District, and it is a paradise for painters. "And yet the fool contends that God is not" as the poem goes. The wonder of Creation. The infinite variety of created things, the vast expanse of the known universe only seen through large telescopes, and things which cannot be seen except through a microscope. Where does space end? The human mind cannot comprehend it any more than it can comprehend God. As created beings with finite minds, we live in time dimension and cannot comprehend eternity. Some scientists argue from the belief that by scientific investigation the mind of humankind will eventually discover the truth about the universe, and that to put the idea of God in the place of undiscovered truth is a cop out. The Christian faith argues from purposeful design in the universe, the laws which govern matter, so that substances behave in predictable ways which can be relied on not to change. Such design requires a creative mind, not something that happens by chance. But the debate about 'God, for and against' will never really get anywhere. The Scripture says - "By faith we understand that the world was created by the word of God."

This means that the Biblical doctrine of creation is based on divine revelation, and understood only from the standpoint of faith. The scientist can be a believer or an unbeliever in this respect because it is a matter of faith and not scientific research. Science may be able to go some way in answering the question *how* the universe was created, but not the question *why*.   Can science explain beauty or love or music except in terms of chemical analysis and mathematical formulae? The Scripture puts it bluntly, "The fool has said in his heart there is no God."

We believe in a faithful Creator. Scientific research is only possible because the physical laws governing the universe do not change. They are there to be explored and used for the benefit of humankind.   We build buildings because we know that materials behave in a certain way; we can rely on it. Cement acts chemically with water to produce concrete, and once set it cannot revert back to being cement, or act in any other way. Clay baked in a kiln at certain temperatures produces hard bricks; it always does. The seasons do not change; they inevitably follow year by year. Farmers can rely on it and make their plans accordingly. God has promised concerning this. He is wholly dependable in everything He says and does. This is why we can depend on His word. What He has promised He will surely perform. Sometimes our faith is tested to see how real it is, when God seems remote and not in control, especially when we are in trouble.   The friends of Jesus, Martha and Mary, couldn't understand why their Lord delayed in coming to their brother who was sick. "Lord, if you had been here, our brother would not have died", they said. But God's ways are not our ways, and His thoughts are not our thoughts.

The atheist stance is, "If God is there let Him prove it." The Scripture says - "Ever since the creation of the world, His invisible nature, namely His eternal power and deity, has been clearly perceived in the things that have been made. So they are without excuse." All ugliness in the world has been produced by sin; people working in opposition to God, or failing to fulfil their true potential. If we defy physical laws, we suffer, and if we defy moral laws we also suffer. Cause and effect. Some things we buy are to be used in accordance with the maker's instructions. If we don't, it goes wrong, or doesn't work as intended. We ignore the instructions at our peril, and it could result in loss and injury, or even death. The instructions are there for our benefit, so that we can get full use and enjoyment from the product. So it is with the word of God, His unchanging laws and decrees. We become whole when Jesus Christ is the centre of our lives, and we submit to His will and His ways, and allow Him full reign. Jesus Christ is Lord of all creation. Through Him all things were made.

Let us give to God all the praise due to His name, Father, Son and Holy Spirit. Faithful Creator, Alpha and Omega, the first and the last, the beginning and the end. He has given us all things, and set our feet upon a rock. Let us pray: Thank you, God our Father for the wonder of your Creation, for the infinite variety and beauty of the things you have made. Thank you for our own creation and preservation and all the blessings of this life. Great is your faithfulness.

The Creation

The Empty Tomb

After the crucifixion of Jesus, the Jewish religious leaders could reasonably have expected the whole following to collapse, never to be heard of again. Such had been the fate of other such movements in the past. Imagine their consternation and confusion then, when the body of Jesus was missing from the tomb. But they would convince themselves that since this could not possibly have been the work of Yahweh, the God of their fathers, the body must have been stolen by the disciples. And this was the story they encouraged to be spread around. Imagine their further consternation and utter confusion, when the disciples themselves began to preach with power and authority, and to heal in the name of Jesus of Nazareth. But they had gone so far down the road of opposition that there was no turning back. Even in the face of overwhelming evidence, the missing body, the power and confidence of the disciples, the healing of the man crippled from birth, they could not accept it. "What are we going to do with these men", they asked themselves. "Everybody living in Jerusalem knows they have done an outstanding miracle, and we cannot deny it. But to stop this thing from spreading any further we must warn these men to speak no longer to anyone in this name." But just as King Canute had no power to keep back the tide, so they could do nothing to prevent the preaching of the gospel in word and action. In the same power across the centuries, that gospel has been, and is being, preached throughout the world, as Christians go out in faith and obedience to their Lord and Saviour's command. The Church in the former Soviet Union, prospered under persecution and could not be stopped. In Africa today, in all the turmoil and trouble of that great continent, the Church is growing fast. Here in the UK the Church has been in decline, but Christians are responding to the call to evangelism through 'Thy Kingdom Come'. Once we were a missionary nation, but now the Church has changed from pastoral care to mission on home territory. Children are growing up relatively ignorant of our Christian heritage, without knowledge of basic Christian teaching and understanding. No wonder there is a moral wilderness, lack of direction, with crime on the increase, drug abuse, sexual abuse, and the rest.

We need that same power and confidence today if we are to combat the spiritual forces of evil which lie behind the moral malaise. We need that same conviction which the Apostles had that salvation is found in no one else. It is in that name of Jesus, and that name alone that we go out, and by which people are brought to God, and healed of all their sins. The Church is still heroic in its mission to preach the gospel, but it seems in many ways, we have settled for the lie that what was seen in the early Church cannot happen any more. We speak the words of faith, but where is the evidence that it makes much difference? Where is the evidence that will convince others that Jesus Christ is Lord? It can only happen when the power of the Holy Spirit is released among God's people, and it can only happen according to our faith. There are great and wonderful promises in the Scriptures, but if we don't really believe them then they are like blank cheques waiting to be filled in and cashed. We believe a legal document when it is signed and sealed, and would pursue it to the highest court in the land. But do we believe the word of God which cannot lie? Do we avail ourselves fully of the means of grace by which we grow and come to maturity in Christ? Preachers should be conscious that when God speaks *through* them, He first must speak *to* them. The chief means of grace are the breaking of bread, study of the word and prayer. If we neglect any of these we are so much poorer and less likely to respond to God's leading in our lives, to reach our full potential as Christians, and therefore less effective in mission and evangelism. Studying the Scriptures in a group is far more beneficial and rewarding than doing it alone. Similarly, learning to pray in a group helps us to tune in to what the Holy Spirit is saying to the whole church, not just to individuals. We can share the mind of Christ. Otherwise to a certain extent we are just play acting, going through the motions, and not fully engaged in the fight.

There is great need in the world today, it hardly needs to be said. The Church of Christ alone can supply the need. During the first world war there was a famous poster of Lord Kitchener with his finger pointing "Britain needs you", and the finger seemed to follow you as you passed by; you couldn't get away from it. We are called to tell others that they need Christ who alone can satisfy all their deepest needs and longings. Let us commit all that we have and are, to Him, to truly be His faithful soldiers and servants to the end of our lives, to the end that His name will be glorified and His kingdom extended.

The Holy Family

The theme is 'The Holy Family' and the significance of the concept of family for us. In an ideal world, children are born to parents who love, and are committed to each other, and who will love and nurture their children, providing guidance, discipline, and freedom to develop to their full potential as mature adults. Sadly, the reality in an imperfect world is often far from the ideal, because in this, as in every other area of life, relationships are flawed by sin, and fall short of the glory of God. Therefore, some children start life with physical and psychological disadvantage, born into unloving, hostile environments, into poverty, disease and starvation. Thus deprived, they decline and die, or are taken into care, or abandoned to fend for themselves like feral cats on city streets. Politicians and sociologists make much of the importance of family life, because they rightly see it as essential to the promotion of a healthy, vigorous, prosperous society.

Christians believe that marriage and family was ordained by God, and seek to promote and encourage permanent stable loving relationships in which people can grow and flourish. As Christians we have been born twice; once physically, and born again spiritually, into the family of God, the Church, the body of Christ. Through faith and trust in our Lord and Saviour, we have received adoption as sons and heirs with God as our Father with whom we can now communicate as His children, using the intimate word 'Abba' (Daddy). All true disciples of whatever denomination, are now our brothers and sisters in Christ, through the fellowship of the Holy Spirit. In this new loving and intimate relationship, we have the means to grow and develop spiritually into full maturity in Christ. The main requirement for health and growth is obedience to our Lord's commands, one of the most important being to love one another. By this, He said, everyone will know that you are my disciples. God's command to all His creatures is to be fruitful and multiply, and to His Church He says - "Go and make disciples of all nations." His desire is that no one should be lost but brought into the household of faith through the knowledge of His love as revealed in His Son. This is the great commission, the prime task of the Church.

It is truly an amazing and wonderful thing that God entrusted His Son to the care of fallible human beings. Human fallibility is revealed in the story from the Gospel of Luke chapter 2. When Jesus was about twelve years of age Joseph and Mary travelled one whole day without knowing that Jesus was missing. They assumed he was with the party. Imagine their anguish mixed with guilt when he was missing for five days; two days travelling and three days searching in Jerusalem. When they found him in the temple, relief and guilt came out in Mary's accusation - "My son, why have you treated us like this?" Jesus appears to have been genuinely surprised. Surely they must have known where he would be? There was a higher calling he was bound to follow, and they should have known that. He grew and developed physically and mentally like any other Jewish boy, but His Father in heaven would have ensured that through the Scriptures His high calling and mission would be revealed to Him. It was to be another 18 years before the start of His short ministry, prompted by the appearance of God's messenger, John the Baptist. The incarnation of the Messiah did not appear in the way the Jews expected. They were awaiting the arrival of a King. Apart from the few to whom His true identity was revealed, the world saw a child born in poverty to parents who were not married, refugees, finally settling in an obscure village, the carpenter's family. After the death of Joseph, the son who would be expected to carry on his father's trade, and with no apparent formal education, became an itinerant preacher with no home or family of His own and claiming to be the Son of God, the Messiah! Then the ultimate disgrace and shame; tried by the highest religious authority in the land, handed over to the hated occupying power, and executed with the lowest common criminals by the most cruel of methods ever devised.

Parents do not own their children; they are entrusted to them by God. Children should obey their parents, but there comes a time when they must make their own decisions. Decisions which may hurt their parents, but which in all conscience, and to be true to themselves, they must make. Parents must be prepared to let their children go, physically and emotionally, if they are to be free. Christian parents have a duty to teach their children the things of God, and to pray for them. Nuclear families can be inward looking, exclusive and self-obsessed. So can the family of God, the Church. If it is not showing love it is not being obedient. It is not being the body of Christ. It is not preaching the gospel. Out there, beyond these walls, is the wider family, the community of which we are a part, and to which we are called to witness; people living in darkness, in ignorance of the love of God in Jesus Christ, and without hope in the world. Our duty to them as servants of God and members of His family, is summed up in the first letter of the Apostle Peter, chapter 2 and verse 9 - "But you are the chosen race, the King's Priests, the holy nation, God's own people, chosen to proclaim the wonderful acts of God who called you out of darkness into His marvellous light."

The Holy Trinity

The doctrine of the Trinity is fundamental to orthodox Christian belief. We state our allegiance to it every Sunday in the words of the Nicene Creed. We have every justification for doing so, and it is well that we do, to keep us from error. Since it is so basic to our faith, is it not surprising that the word Trinity is nowhere to be found in Scripture? This is a fact that Jehovah's Witnesses are quick to point out. Yet the doctrine is implied throughout the Bible from the first chapter of Genesis, becoming clearer and clearer as an image emerges, culminating in the words of our Lord Jesus Christ to His disciples, just before His ascension into heaven to – "Go, and make disciples of all nations, baptizing them in the name of the Father, and of the Son, and of the Holy Spirit." Denial of the doctrine reduces our Lord to being merely a man, and even a 'god', whatever that means, and the Spirit to an impersonal force which moves God's servants to do His will. It's like science fiction, as in the popular film 'Star Wars', when the saviour-like character, Obi Wan Kenobi says, "May the Force be with you." This is not the Saviour and Spirit we encounter in the word of God from Genesis to Revelation. The three-fold nature of God is apparent throughout, and not the least concerning the baptism of Jesus in the River Jordan where we see the Father speaking from heaven, and the Holy Spirit descending on Jesus in the form of a dove. The Scriptures reveal the creative fullness of the Godhead, able to communicate both within Himself, and without, to the whole creation. According to Jehovah's Witnesses, God is a solitary being from eternity, unrevealed and unknown. No one has existed as His equal to reveal Him.

"Explain the Trinity", the priest said to the little boy in the Bible class; "Three in One and One in Three", replied the boy. "I don't understand", said the priest. "You're not supposed to understand", said the boy, "It's a mystery." Yes, it is a mystery, which we poor mortals struggle to comprehend. Yet, if we take a look at ourselves, we see a reflection of the threefold nature of our Creator. We are complex creatures comprising body, mind, and spirit, all essential to our unique individual personalities, capable of communicating not only with each other, but with our God, and being ourselves creative. Perhaps this gives some insight into the words of God recorded in Genesis chapter 1, "Let us make man in our image, after our likeness."

Most people, when they look at the created world, are amazed at its complexity and diversity. The infinite variety of plants and creatures is staggering. Yet, all things in their incredible diversity, are interdependent, all needing each other, and with common basic needs to survive. So we can say that there is a unity in diversity in creation which reflects the nature of the Godhead. I think that part of humankind's problem in coming to terms with the idea of the Trinity, is that we like to box God in to the limits where we can control Him. It is much too disturbing to have Him breaking out in an uncontrolled way. Not knowing what He is going to get up to next. Nowhere is this true than in the Church, and in particular, the Church of England. We do, of course, accept the doctrine of the Trinity, and in our worship, unity in diversity, but working it out in practice is difficult. There has long been within the Church, three traditions, broadly described as High Church or Anglo-Catholic, Liberal, and Low Church or Evangelical. A simplification of the main themes of these three traditions would be, Ceremonial, Reason, and Authority of Scripture. Naturally enough, people tend to congregate where they feel most comfortable, and worship with like minded people within the same tradition. This has tended to fragment the Church, and create problems for Archbishops and Bishops in trying to maintain unity in diversity. Being human, we tend to feel that our particular way is best, and that somehow the others haven't got it quite right. The fact is, of course, that no one tradition has a monopoly of the truth, and that each has a great deal to learn from the others, if only we were open to receive it.

Our preferences make for difficulties when they conflict within the same congregation, and very real divisions and rifts may occur. Our faith and love can be tested to the limit under such conditions, and sometimes sadly, results in people leaving a church to find another where they will feel more at home. Some accommodation on all sides is necessary without compromising our conscience before God. We have a God who can communicate with those who are open to new ideas, to creative ways of spreading the gospel, and looking for the Holy Spirit to guide and direct. We may feel led in a certain way and come to the point where we have to say, with Martin Luther, "Here I stand, I can do no other." The psalmist says - "Behold, how good and pleasant it is when brothers dwell in unity." Our Lord's command to His disciples was that they should love one another. The Holy Trinity speaks to us of unity in diversity, the richness and abundance of God's creation. Let us pray for wisdom and understanding and openness to the Holy Spirit, so that we do not create God in our own image, but allow Him to express Himself among us in all His fullness.

The Life of Faith

"We walk by faith and not by sight." So says the Apostle Paul in his second letter to the church at Corinth. So what does it mean? It means that we act according to what we believe, not relying on the evidence of our eyes. It is a matter of insight rather than eyesight. We may think we have very little faith, but we all use faith every day. In fact, life would be impossible without it. We sit on a chair, or lie on a bed, in faith that it will support our weight. We believe it will and act on our belief. Our action validates our belief, makes it real. We get on a train or bus in faith that it will take us to where we want to go, and get us there safely. We don't question the ability of the driver. We trust the reputation of the train or bus company. That's faith. We trust the food we eat in a restaurant. We trust the chef, even though we can't see him or her, nor the state of the kitchen. Some years ago I went to measure up a restaurant for the purpose of converting it to become a dry cleaner's shop. I made the mistake of having lunch before surveying the kitchen. Had I done so, I would never have eaten in that restaurant. My faith on this occasion was totally misplaced. Sight killed it.

The Word of God is quite clear about what faith is. In the eleventh chapter of the letter to the Hebrews, we read that - "Faith is being sure of what we hope for, and certain of what we do not see." It is not vague longings. There is assurance and certainty about it. In that sense it is the gift of God. If we do not have it, we can only desire it and pray for it. Some things in which we put our faith are not all that certain. Human nature being what it is, trains, planes and buses do have accidents; some people die from food poisoning. But that does not stop us travelling and eating. We still have sufficient faith to keep going, placing our lives in the hands of others, about most of whom we know nothing. We are here today because of faith, no matter how small or feeble we may feel that to be. Our relationship to God does not depend on the strength of our faith, but on the reliability and faithfulness of God, the faithful Creator, who cannot lie, and who always keeps His promises. What He promises He will surely perform. Faith in God through His Son is never misplaced no matter how weak. One woman merely touched the hem of His cloak and she was healed. She acted on the belief that here was a person who could heal. We act on our belief by coming to church this morning to worship God, and to bring a child to be baptised into the fellowship of His Church. Our faith is made real by our action. We commit ourselves to a public confession by being here, part of the worshipping community.

There is no stereotype Christian. We all come for various reasons, from different backgrounds and viewpoints, each being completely unique and infinitely precious in the sight of God. This is brought out sharply by the contrasting characters of Daniel and Zacchaeus. Daniel was a prophet, a man of great intelligence and outstanding wisdom, but taken from Judah in captivity to the Persian capital, Babylon. Promoted to high office because of his outstanding gifts, he was not deterred from praying to his God in spite of being forbidden to do so. By faith he was not afraid of being torn apart by lions, but looked beyond that to his God who would deliver him if he remained faithful. God honoured Daniel's faithfulness, because after a night in the lion's den, "no kind of hurt was found upon him, because he trusted in his God." Zacchaeus who lived in the time of Jesus, was a totally different character. No doubt intelligent, but a man on the make, a collaborator with the occupying power, the Romans. A tax collector who creamed off funds into his own pocket. Rich, powerful, and hated by the people. But he had a determination and desire to see Jesus. Being small in stature, he was not deterred by not being able to see above the heads of the crowds, and when given the opportunity, welcomed Jesus into his home and into his life. From that day he was a changed person, giving half of his money to the poor, and repaying four times over, those he had cheated. Salvation had come to his house that day.

Daniel was saved from the lions; Zacchaeus was saved from his evil ways; and we are saved from our sins through faith in Jesus Christ. As Paul puts it - "Since we are justified by faith, we have peace with God through our Lord Jesus Christ" - *Romans 5:1*. Justified means declared or shown to be free from blame or guilt. This is the good news! This is the gospel. This is what a sin-sick world needs to hear. God shows His love for us in that while we were yet sinners, Christ died for us - *Romans 5:8*. So let us act according to what we believe, making progress in our life of faith, and in all that we do and say, proclaiming the message of reconciliation.

The Lord's Prayer Part 1

The necessity of prayer is based on helplessness and faith, and that in essence it is nothing more than giving Jesus access to our needs. Prayer is also a powerful weapon in the spiritual battle in which the followers of Jesus are engaged. We acknowledge difficulties because of our natural reluctance to pray, and because the adversary attacks us at this point. There are common mistakes that we make, but we should not be put off by the difficulties. Practice and perseverance are needed. The disciples were aware of the importance of prayer, because they saw their Lord gave it priority in His life. He often went away to pray to His Father, sometimes spending all night in prayer. So they asked Him, "Lord, teach us to pray." - *Luke 11:1*. Look up Matthew 6:5 to 14 for Jesus' teaching on prayer, and the model prayer:

> Our Father in heaven, hallowed be your name,
> Your kingdom come, your will be done,
> On earth as it is in heaven.
> Give us today our daily bread.
> Forgive us our sins,
> As we forgive those who sin against us.
> Lead us not into temptation,
> But deliver us from evil.
> For the kingdom, the power and the glory
> Are yours, now and for ever.
> Amen.

The prayer Jesus taught the disciples was designed to be a pattern of how to talk to God, not to be used as a prayer in itself. It consists of the Invocation, six petitions and the Doxology. The first three petitions refer to God's name, kingdom and will. The last three petitions refer to people's need of bread, forgiveness and victory. The Doxology is a threefold declaration concerning God's kingdom, power and glory. Let's look at the model prayer phrase by phrase.

Our Father in Heaven

Intended to produce in us a sense of intimacy, and a feeling of reverence. The words, "Our Father", express the closeness of our relationship with God. Security and contentment. Just as children in a human family, confident that their father's concern and interest takes in with one large embrace, all the small and great things in their lives. Love will not diminish because of disobedience. Dad may discipline, but as a loving father, his heart yearns for the re-establishment of a close and warm relationship. Only believers in Jesus can come to God as Father with this same assurance. God shows a loving concern for all humankind, but the only people qualified to say, "Our Father in Heaven", are those who have been redeemed through faith in Jesus Christ. There is a need for reverence. The feeling of closeness must never lead to disrespect or an overly-familiar attitude. God is in Heaven; we are on earth. He is infinite in holiness and power; we are sinful and weak.

Hallowed be your Name

Let your name be honoured above all other names. Leads to praising God for His majesty and glory. Our priority in prayer is to glorify God. Praise delivers us from self-centredness. To hallow means to reverence, sanctify or keep holy. See *Exodus 3:14* - "I AM WHO I AM." If we over-emphasise His Fatherhood, we will tend to drag Him down to our level. If we over-concentrate on His holiness, we will not be able to lift ourselves up to His.

<u>Your kingdom come</u>

A longing for that day when the rule of God will be universally acknowledged. We live in a world marred by sin, under the influence of Satan, the god of this age. Misery, disease, and death, injustice and evil. One day our Lord Jesus will return and establish His reign. We yearn for the time foretold by the prophet Jeremiah chapter 23 verses 5 and 6 - "The days are coming," declares the Lord, "when I will raise up to David a righteous Branch, a King who will reign wisely and do what is just and right in the land. In his days Judah will be saved and Israel will live in safety. This is the name by which he will be called: The Lord Our Righteousness." *Revelation 22:20* - "Even so, come Lord Jesus." We want the Lord's will to be done here and now; that men and women everywhere acknowledge Jesus Christ as Lord.

The Lord's Prayer Part 2

Part 2 concerns the petitions and the Doxology.

The first three petitions refer to God's name, kingdom and will. The last three petitions refer to people's need of bread, forgiveness and victory. The Doxology is a threefold declaration concerning God's kingdom, power and glory.

<u>Give us today our Daily Bread</u>

God cares not only about us as spiritual people, but as those who have physical needs as well. Jesus knew what it was like to be hungry, thirsty and tired. His obvious concern for the physical needs of others comes out strongly in the story of the feeding of the five thousand in the Gospels. Love has to give. God is love - *1 John 4:8*. God's gifts are good, and He gives to those who ask - "If you then, being evil, know how to give gifts to your children; how much more will the heavenly Father give good gifts to those who ask him" - *Matthew 7:11*. We are to live in conscious dependence on God, and be willing to live one day at a time. Daily rations, allotment for a single day. We don't need to worry about tomorrow's bread. God provided bread, called manna, in the desert for His people Israel. In *Proverbs 30:8,9 we read* - "Keep falsehood and lies far from me; give me neither poverty nor riches, but give me only my daily bread. Otherwise I may have too much and disown you and say, 'Who is the Lord?' Or I may become poor and steal, and so dishonour the name of my God." "Bread" includes all our material needs, and also includes spiritual provision. Jesus is the Bread of Life - *John 6:35*

<u>Forgive us our sins</u>

"If we confess our sins, He is faithful and just to forgive our sins, and cleanse us from all unrighteousness" - *1 John 1:19*. Is it easy, to own up to being wrong? We excuse or justify ourselves. To some who were confident of their own righteousness and looked down on everybody else, Jesus told a parable concerning a self righteous Pharisee and a humble tax collector: *Luke 18:9-12*. There are two elements to forgiveness; receiving it and giving it. This forces us to examine our attitudes to those around us. Our natural reaction is to want to get even; we find it hard to forgive, and we bear a grudge. It is only when we consider the debt we owe to Jesus Christ, that we shall truly appreciate why we must forgive.

<u>Lead us not into temptation</u>
When tempted, no one should say, "God is tempting me." For God cannot be tempted by evil, nor does He tempt anyone; but each one is tempted when, by his own evil desire, he is dragged away and enticed - *James 1: 13,14*. We should pray in advance that the Father will shield and deliver us from missing our way, and plunging ourselves into disaster. We need deliverance from the world, the flesh, and the devil. <u>The world</u>. We are pressurised to conform to the world. "Do not conform any longer to the pattern of this world, but be transformed by the renewing of your mind" - *Romans 12:2*. We are tempted to compromise, sit on the fence. "Am I now trying to win the approval of men, or of God? Or am I trying to please men? If I were still trying to please men, I would not be a servant of Christ" - *Galatians 1:10*. <u>The flesh</u>. The spirit is willing but the flesh is weak. "So if you think you are standing firm, be careful that you don't fall" - *1 Corinthians 10:12*. Problems of the flesh – over-indulgence, laziness, indiscipline, over-working, pre-occupation with appearance etc. <u>The devil.</u> "Put on the full armour of God so that you can take your stand against the devil's schemes. For our struggle is not against flesh and blood, but against the powers of this

dark world and against the spiritual forces of evil in the heavenly realms" - *Ephesians 6:11,12*. "Submit to God, resist the devil and he will flee from you" - *James 4:7*.

<u>For the kingdom, the power and the glory are yours, now and for ever</u>

David praised the Lord in the presence of the whole assembly, saying - "Praise be to you, O Lord, God of our father Israel, from everlasting to everlasting. Yours O Lord is the greatness and the power and the glory and the majesty and the splendour, for everything in heaven and earth is yours. Yours O Lord is the kingdom; you are exalted as head over all. Wealth and honour come from you; you are the ruler of all things. In your hands are strength and power to exalt and give strength to all. Now, our God, we give you thanks, and praise your glorious name" - *1 Chronicles 29:10-13*. Remind yourself that God reigns over everything. Begin the new day with boldness and expectancy. You are the son or daughter of the King.

The Meaning of Law

On one occasion I was driving into Newcastle and had nearly reached the end of the Coast Road, when I noticed a police car behind me flashing for me to pull over and stop. I had not reduced speed from the 70mph limit to the 50mph limit which is clearly marked. The fact that most other drivers appeared to be doing the same was beside the point. I had broken the law and was being brought to book. The police officer was my judge and jury, and I could have been fined and incurred penalty points. In the event the police officer was merciful, and let me off with a caution, for which I was extremely thankful. The law is there for a purpose, in this case for the safety of all road users in reducing the speed of traffic approaching a controlled road junction. In breaking the law, I was putting not only myself, but others at risk. This should be the prime motive for obedience and not fear of detection. Fear of the law may produce the desired effect, but it is not the ideal. In all areas of life, consideration and love for others should dictate behaviour, not fear of being found out and punished for wrongdoing. Laws are good and necessary otherwise there would be chaos. The definition of law is, 'a rule or set of rules instituted by Act of Parliament, custom or practice, in order to punish those who offend the convention of society; and law and order is the policy of strict enforcement of the law.' There is also the law of nature which is a generalisation based on a recurring fact or event. The law of gravity is an example, and one which applies on earth, but not, as we now know, in space. We know where we are with the law of gravity, but just imagine what would happen if we couldn't rely on it, and things and people suddenly started floating about or disappearing into space! As well as physical laws upon which we can rely, God has given us moral laws, the breaking of which produces certain results. These are intended for our greatest good, and breaking them can bring chaos and misery.

The truth is that in our fallen state with our sinful nature, we cannot keep God's laws. God knows that we cannot keep them, but the trouble is, we do not know it. Our pride rebels against the idea that we are helpless and hopeless, and insists that if we tried a little harder, we could do it. In that frame of mind, we miss the whole point of the gospel. People who believe that they are good and have done no one any harm, are in a spiritually dangerous condition, because they will never see the need of a Saviour. Man in the gutter gazes up at the unreachable stars. If he stands on the highest peak of human achievement and excellence, he is still gazing up at the stars, way out of reach. That is how far we fall short. The "wretched man" of Romans chapter 7, tried to meet the claims of God's law himself, and that was the cause of his trouble. The repeated use of the word "I" in this chapter gives the clue to the failure. He thought God was asking him to keep the law, so of course he was trying to do so, whereas God was asking no such thing of him. He needed to be brought to the realisation of his innate helplessness. The point is illustrated by Watchman Nee in his book 'The Normal Christian Life'. Some young men went swimming in a river and one got into difficulties with cramp and was drowning. On the bank stood a strong swimmer to whom the others looked to rescue the drowning man. But he did nothing. He just stood looking on. It was not until the man was sinking that the strong swimmer dived in and brought him to the river bank. The rescuer was taken to task by his friends for not going in earlier. "Had I gone in earlier", he said, "he would have clutched me so fast that both of us would have gone under. A drowning man cannot be saved until he is utterly exhausted and ceases to make the slightest effort to save himself." Do you see the point? God is waiting until we are at the end of our resources, and can do nothing more for ourselves.

This is the truth of our condition, and until we fully accept the fact, we shall constantly be trying to please God by our own efforts. The man in Romans 7 is brought to the point where light breaks through and he says - "Wretched man that I am, who will deliver me from this body of death?" He recognises that he needs someone to deliver him from this condition, and he concludes: "Thanks be to God through Jesus Christ our Lord." We did not look to our own efforts for forgiveness; we looked to Jesus Christ on the cross. Much of the trouble in the Church, I believe, arises out of failure at this point. Christ is the one who does it all. It is finished. We have been restored to a position of grace, which means God does something for me. Law means I do something for God, and the law exposes my true nature.   The law has served its purpose. It has been our schoolmaster to bring us to Christ, that in us He Himself may fulfil it. Because only He can.

The More Excellent Way

In his first letter to the church at Corinth, the Apostle Paul says that the more excellent way is love. Pontius Pilate asked Jesus the profound question, "what is truth?" He didn't wait for an answer, presumably because he thought that no one could answer it. The question today, however, is not "what is truth?", but "what is love?" An equally profound question you may think. So where do we look for an answer? One of the tabloid newspapers used to run a cartoon series called 'Love Is', with captions such as, "Love is washing his socks", or, "Love is making her a cup of tea". Well, I suppose that goes some way towards it, but if we want something with more substance, let's look at what God says that love is, through His servant Paul. In his first letter to the church at Corinth chapter 13 and verses 4 to 7, this is what Paul says - "Love is patient; love is kind and envies no one. Love is never boastful, nor conceited nor rude; never selfish, not quick to take offence. Love keeps no score of wrongs; does not gloat over other men's sins, but delights in the truth. There is nothing love cannot face; there is no limit to its faith, its hope and its endurance."

This then, is the more excellent way. But more excellent than what? Paul had previously been describing God's spiritual gifts to the Church. We may possess all these gifts, and certainly we need them, but if we do not have love, they are of no value. Paul says we might as well bang a gong or clang a cymbal, for all the good it will do. Many years ago, a man came into my office in London and began to recite verse after verse of Scripture, just like a machine, as if someone had switched him on. He may have had a gift of knowledge, but there was no love there. The effect was pathetic. He might just as well have come in banging a gong.

Some may think that the spiritual gifts don't apply in the Church today, and that all we need is love. If that is so, then how do we measure up to Paul's description of love? We may feel that on our best days we do reasonably well, but what about every day and all the time? We know that most of the time we fall far short of that standard. Yet God requires that quality of love towards Him, and to our neighbours. This quality of love requires supernatural grace, and it needed one of the least common words in classical Greek to describe it. The word is 'agape' (pronounced agapay), which expresses that highest and noblest form of love which sees something infinitely precious in its object. It is the love which God Himself shows towards us, and is the fruit of the Holy Spirit. It produces that quality which enables us to love the unlovely, and even to love our enemies.

Jesus preferred to speak of the ideal relationship of man to God, not in terms of love, but in terms of faith. Agape love finds its true expression, not in feelings, but in obedience to God; faith in action. So it is, that we are enabled by the grace of God, to show love towards those we naturally dislike, and even those who hate us. This is clearly contrary to human nature, and brings home forcefully to us our need. We do good to others because we see in them those for whom Christ died, and because we see in them, Christ Himself. There is a great need for love in the world today where we see so much hatred and violence. Without love, personalities are warped and twisted, where they are used and abused and exploited. Jesus commands His disciples to love one another.   It is this love within the Church, above all things, that is the sign to the outside world of the reality of Christian discipleship. "By this shall all men know that you are my disciples, if you have love, one for another." So goes the well known hymn. People are dying through lack of love, looking for the quality of love that only God can give through His Church, empowered by the Holy Spirit. Jesus promised that His followers would do the things that He was doing, and even greater things. In the early Church many signs and wonders were done through the Apostles.

Is God's power diminished today? Our Lord Jesus is the same yesterday, today and forever. It is as always, a question of our faith. The need is great, "the fields are white for the harvest" - *John 4:35*. Our God is calling us to go, out and preach the gospel. People need to know that God loves them, and that Jesus died for them. It means dying to self interest, putting aside rights and privileges. Our Lord Jesus made Himself of no reputation, and came in the form of a servant. As we seek to go out in response to our Lord's command, let us cry out to Him with a deep yearning for the fullness of the Holy Spirit, so that we may overflow with love. It will be in the overflowing that people of our parish will be blessed. St. John sums it up in these words - "This is how we know what love is: Jesus Christ laid down His life for us. And we ought to lay-down our lives for our brothers" - *1 John 3:16*

The Offering of Life

The little boy gazed at the Sanctuary Lamp during a very long sermon. After a while he turned to his mother and said, "When the red light turns to green, can we go?" Well, ten minutes is the tolerance limit. After that, is what one preacher called 'injury time'. It is important to be clear about what our main purpose is as Christians, and in particular as the body of Christ, the Church. It is to make disciples by our witness in word and action. That was our Lord's command to His disciples, and for which they received the power of the Holy Spirit on the day of Pentecost. If we accept this to be true, then it follows that all we undertake here in the name of Jesus Christ must be geared to that purpose. "Be fruitful and multiply" is a principle of life for all of God's creation, and it applies to the things that are not seen just as much as the things that are seen. This is illustrated most graphically in the parable of the sower and the seed, the meaning of which Jesus fully explained to His disciples. What does this require of us here to enable God's purpose to be fulfilled in and through us? I believe several things; but the most important is to really get hold of the fact that we are not merely a collection of individuals who happen to meet together for worship on Sundays, but that in Christ we are one body, the Church. We do not all have the same function, but have different gifts to be used for the benefit of the whole Church. It is an individual and corporate responsibility to ensure that the Church works as a fully co-ordinated, healthy body. Commitment is the essential ingredient in any team, working together for a common goal. Any dissension or dissatisfaction in a team, and murmuring against the management, is destructive and self-defeating. The same applies to the Church. It is up to us individually to offer ourselves to God for His purpose, to find our proper place in the body, and for which we have been especially gifted by Him.

This is the ideal; how it should be, and what we should be working towards. It starts with the offering of a single life, described by the Apostle Paul as 'a living sacrifice'. A definition of sacrifice, apart from ritual killing, is the surrender of something of value as a means of gaining something more desirable, or preventing some evil. We are exhorted to "present our bodies as a living sacrifice, holy and acceptable to God." We do not appease a wrathful God in this way, because the sacrifice for sin has already been offered and accepted by God. As the writer of Hebrews puts it - Jesus Christ "appeared once for all at the end of the ages to put away sin by the sacrifice of Himself." - *Hebrews 9:26.* Notice that important phrase "once for all", a single act, for everyone, for all time, never to be repeated. In the words of our Lord Jesus from the cross - "It is finished."

All that we are required to do then, is to offer our bodies as a living sacrifice, and continually offer up a sacrifice of praise and thanksgiving. That is the hoped for response to the demonstration of God's love we have been shown in His Son. The prophet Isaiah made this response when he saw the Lord high and lifted up. He heard the voice of the Lord say - "Whom shall I send, and who will go for us.", and to which the prophet's response was - "Here am I, send me.". The Lord's acceptance was immediate - "Go and tell this people", He said. We are the ones commissioned to "Go and tell this people"; in our case meaning our friends and neighbours, those with whom we come into contact day by day. Whatever they may appear to be, without Christ they are oppressed, wretched, blind and lame, and without hope in the world. The last world war effort demanded commitment and sacrifice even unto death, and the laying aside of all personal ambition and worldly gain. The aim was to create a better, freer world, to rid it of tyranny and slavery. This is God's aim through His Church, to set people free in body, mind and spirit, in every aspect of their being.

If we are to be effective in this purpose, we must lay aside every weight and the sin that does so easily beset us, and look unto Jesus. It demands commitment and working together in love and fellowship, setting aside party spirit and petty bickering. God has called us to this task. It is inspired by the Holy Spirit who also equips us for it. It calls for living sacrifice, the offering of life. This is not a once for all thing, although there may be an initial prompting to positive commitment. It is something we do on a daily basis at the beginning of each new day which is complete in itself having a birth, a life and a death, and is new every morning. Prayer and Bible study are essential if we are to share a common vision. Knowledge of God's word is necessary for spiritual maturity. The early Church devoted themselves to the Apostles' teaching, fellowship, and the breaking of bread, and prayer; and they turned the world upside down. Perhaps this can be summed up in *1 Peter 4:7-11* - "You must lead an ordered and sober life, given to prayer. Above all keep your love for one another at full strength. Whatever gift each of you may have received, use it in service to one another. In all things so act that the glory may be God's through Jesus Christ; to Him belong glory and power for ever and ever."

The Problem of Doubt

To be called 'a doubting Thomas' is derogatory. Does the original Thomas deserve to be remembered in this way? Some people demand proof before they will accept anything, but if you behaved like that about everything, then life would become impossible. Without faith of some kind we wouldn't survive one day. Faith in the bus driver or the train driver, faith in the cook who provides our meals, faith in the very air we breathe into our lungs. It is not blind faith. We have reasonable expectation from experience that all will be well, but there is a risk factor. Human error occurs every day, and we read or hear about it in the media. But our faith extends beyond reason to suppose that it won't happen to us. It just happens to other people. The whole of life is a risk, but in the balance of probabilities, most people exercise their faith in making the most of it and being positive. Christians are required to walk by faith and not by sight. But our faith goes beyond the natural to the supernatural, to life beyond death, to belief and trust in a loving Creator who supremely has our wellbeing at heart, who loves us with an everlasting love. In various ways God has touched our hearts, assured us of His love through the life, death and resurrection of His Son, and has received our response of faith and trust in Him. Yet we are prone to doubting, to negative thinking; part of the result of our fallen nature. It was doubt that the enemy of souls used to bring about the original fall of humanity. He confused the woman by misquoting God's command about the fruit of the trees in the garden, but when corrected, went on to plant the seed of doubt about the consequences of disobedience. Confusion and doubt caused wrong action, and a rift was made between a righteous Creator and fallen creatures, no longer able to dwell together in trust and harmony.

What we know of the disciple Thomas is recorded only in the Gospel of John, where he is referred to three times. The first in connection with Lazarus, the brother of Mary and Martha. The second in connection with Jesus preparing His disciples for His departure from them. The third and most well known occasion of the resurrection appearance of Jesus in the upper room. On the first occasion, after learning of the death of Lazarus, he said bravely to the other disciples, "Let us go also that we may die with him." But in saying this, he ignored a strong intimation from Jesus that He was going to wake Lazarus up from death. Thomas would have been a witness to the actual restoration of life to Lazarus. On the second occasion, we see him questioning Jesus about His imminent departure. He said: "Lord we do not know where you are going, so how can we know the way?" This prompted the well known powerful answer, "I am the Way, the Truth, and the Life. No one can come to the Father except through me." The third occasion sees Thomas unwilling or unable to accept the testimony of his fellow disciples that they had seen the risen Lord, and spoken to Him. So what do we learn of his character from this, and what does it teach us today? First he was not lacking in courage. He appeared to have no fear of death, but his faith in Jesus did not extend to believing He could raise the dead. He was not afraid to ask direct questions, but was reluctant to accept the testimony of his friends. Although he had witnessed numerous miracles, and in particular the raising of Lazarus, his questioning mind would not allow belief in the resurrection of Jesus without concrete evidence. We see in the way Jesus dealt with Thomas that He knew and understood him, and lovingly sought to encourage faith in him. In the end the wonderful response of Thomas, "My Lord and my God", was not a result of his demand to feel the crucifixion wounds, but the realisation that Jesus knew what was in his heart. A similar response had come from the disciple Nathanael when he asked Jesus, "How do you know me?" Jesus reply revealed personal knowledge of Nathanael's heart that only God could know, prompting the declaration of faith, "You are the Son of God; you are the King of Israel."

The fact is that we are all prone to doubts of one kind or another in relation to our faith, because we are faced with problems every day which test our faith. They raise questions in our minds to which we may have no satisfactory answers. The danger for us is when we question the very foundation, rather than the superstructure. Then the whole building may collapse and we are left standing battered and bleeding in the rubble. The fact of the resurrection is such a foundation. The problem for us is to keep our questions, doubts and faith in balance, so that we make actual spiritual progress, and our doubts don't impede our effective witness. The closer we keep to Jesus and the more we get to know Him, the less room there will be for doubting. Ignorance breeds confusion, and confusion leads to doubts. Knowledge is gained by prayer and the diligent study of the word of God, because we stand on the promises of God. It was the key of promise that released Christian and Hopeful from Doubting Castle, kept by Giant Despair.

We walk by faith and not by sight, because we are those commended by Jesus to Thomas: "Have you believed because you have seen me? Blessed are those who have not seen and yet believe." Are we doubting His presence with us? Reach for the key of promise, "In everything God works for good to those who love Him, who are called according to His purpose." Unlock the door and walk free.

The Remnant of Israel

The stage of world history has seen many men and women of faith, of great spiritual stature, with the power of God in them. Some have been held hostage in captivity for many years for political or religious reasons. Their faith in Jesus Christ has sustained them throughout their ordeal. The Lord, in His mercy has looked with compassion on them, strengthened and protected them, supplied their needs and enfolded them with His love.   In spite of physical incarceration, there is a sense in which they have always been free. As our Lord Jesus Himself said - "If the Son makes you free, you will be free indeed." Terry Waite was such a person held captive in isolation for many years. After being freed from prison at last, his only words of reproach for his captors were these - "It is wrong to hold people in such a way. Those who do it fall well below civilised standards of behaviour." This mild understatement, this generous forbearance in the face of such horrific injury to himself, tells us a lot about the strength of the Judeo-Christian tradition of which Terry Waite is such a fine example. It is a tradition which stresses the creative value of suffering and provides many instances of its redemptive quality, and which, with even greater emphasis insists on the need to forgive.

Abraham was such a man of faith, of great spiritual stature, and one to whom God promised that all the nations of the earth would be blessed through him. The Apostle Paul says this of him - "Abraham believed God and it was reckoned to him as righteousness." Through Isaac, Jacob and his twelve sons, the descendants of Abraham multiplied and became a nation – Israel. Under Moses, God delivered Israel from slavery in Egypt, and through much suffering, established them in the land He had promised them.   God chose them to be His special people in a binding contract or covenant. He showed them that He loved them, that they could trust Him for all their needs, and looked for a response of love. But they rebelled against Him, broke His laws, and suffered the consequences of their own actions. Yet in each generation there was a remnant who remained faithful, the true descendants of Abraham.

In Jesus' day, the Jewish religious leaders were proud to be descended from Abraham, and believed that on the basis of birth alone, they would inherit all the promises of God. They were not at all pleased to be shown by Jesus that it was not a question of birth-right, but a matter of inheriting the righteousness of Abraham. Their history and traditions had blinded them to the true purposes of God, the covenant of love, and they failed to recognize their Messiah when He came among them. Yet, as in previous generations, there was a remnant watching and waiting for God's promise, and ready to receive Him. It is those who walk by faith, and not according to the works of the law who are the true Israel of God, whether they are Jew or Gentile. As the Apostle Paul tells us - "It is people of faith who are the descendants of Abraham. If you are Christ's, you are Abraham's offspring, and heirs according to promise." So it is that the promises of God are open to everyone who will receive them by faith. "There is neither Jew nor Greek", says Paul - "For you are all one in Christ Jesus."

Where do we stand in this matter? It really comes down to this – are we trying to please God by our own efforts, i.e. by the works of the law? If so, then we are on the wrong track, for the Scripture says, "All who rely on the works of the law are under a curse." - *Galatians 3:10.* Or have we put our whole trust in Christ, and in His finished work for us on the cross? If we could make it by our own actions, then it would not have been necessary for Christ to die. As Paul puts it: "If justification were through the law, then Christ died to no purpose." Jesus came to set us free. Many churchgoing people have crippling images of God which prevent them from turning to Him with enough love and trust to enable their liberation to take effect. Their Christian faith has not really become "good news" for them. They are still living under the law. If we are like that, then we have nothing to say to those who are outside the Church. The core of renewal in the Church is surrendering ourselves completely into the hands of Jesus Christ and allowing ourselves to be filled and led by the Holy Spirit.

Commitment is really like a marriage vow. We love, and so we can make the promise. The contract is made and cannot be undone in the sight of God. He takes us at our word, but very often we back down on our commitment. It is something we need to renew every day as we confess our sins. His mercies are new every morning! In the end it does not rest on us. God Himself does it all through us as we make ourselves available to Him. It is not ability He wants, but availability. All the glory must go to Him. If we are successful in our own right then we receive the glory, and that is wrong. In all things He must have pre-eminence. What can we do?

1. Recognise and acknowledge our helplessness before God.
2. Desire to be used by Him in His service.
3. Offer ourselves to Him on a daily basis.

Let us celebrate our freedom in the gospel. To God be the glory, great things He has done!

The Serving Community

When the second world war ended in 1945, I was fourteen years old, and 4 years later was conscripted into the army on National Service. For reasons I was never able to understand, I was sent to the Far East, and spent 4 weeks on a troopship bound for Singapore. This was just 4 years after the Japanese had unconditionally surrendered, and by that time there was very little evidence they had ever been there. Some of those who suffered as prisoners of the Japanese find it difficult if not impossible to forgive, because of the barbaric treatment they received, even if there was an apology and compensation from Japan. Now there were other problems to contend with. The Chinese Communists were causing havoc and mayhem in the Malayan jungle. Infantry units were being trained in Singapore before being sent up country into the jungle to combat the terrorists.

As Christians, our Lord Jesus tells us to love our enemies, and do good to those who hate us. Only God can bring about true healing which is impossible, humanly speaking. Years ago we had in this church, a prayer support group for the Overseas Missionary Fellowship working in Japan, where through OMF, local groups of Japanese people were brought to faith in Jesus Christ. Japanese Samurai were a warrior caste dedicated to a lifetime of loyalty and service to their feudal overlord. The name Samurai means 'one who serves'. A dispute arose between the disciples of Jesus about which of them was the greatest. Jesus said to them, "Who is greater, the one who sits at the table, or the one who serves? It is the one who sits at the table. But I am among you as one who serves." The sorts of service rendered by the Samurai and our Lord Jesus are worlds apart, but the expression is a noble one. A servant in the

Scriptures is a person at the disposal of another; a worker who belongs to a master. Loyalty and service are attitudes and actions which reflect the actual or perceived will of the master being served, whether benign or evil. Actions will therefore be largely dictated by the nature of the master, his philosophy and ambitions. In Nazi Germany, for example, the Fuhrer dictator, Adolf Hitler, and in Japan at war, the Emperor god, Hirohito. Loyalty and service to these masters led to the horrors of the Holocaust, and the Burma railway slave camps.

The Master to whom we owe loyalty and service, is none other than the God of all creation, and whose name is Love, and who is faithful and just in all His ways. We are servants at the disposal of our heavenly Father, and constantly seek His will through prayer, and the study of His word. He requires the willing offering of ourselves in His service. We do not receive wages, but gifts, constantly flowing from His loving hand, resulting in the response of thanksgiving and praise, and being ever more willing to carry out His will. In spite of his many failings, King David truly loved God, and tried to serve him. He recognised that all that he was and possessed, was God given, and he was full of thanks and praise, as we know from the Psalms. He gave God the glory for everything. He wanted to build a Temple and provided resources for it, but it would be constructed by his son, Solomon. As King, he had given a lead and example, and now posed the question: Who is willing to consecrate himself to the Lord?" The leaders, officers, commanders, officials, gave willingly. David rejoiced and praised the Lord in the words we use in church when the offerings are presented, "Yours Lord, is the greatness, the power and the glory, the splendour and the majesty; for everything in heaven and on earth is yours. All things come from you, and of your own do we give you."

Our Father has held nothing back from us, giving His most treasured possession, His only beloved Son, his very self, to suffer utmost degradation and torture at the hands of men. Our response of love is giving all that we are and possess in His service; our time, talents, treasure. It is both a personal and collective response, because we are all members one of another, the body of Christ. Our giving is not to the institution, the Church, but an offering to God. Any meanness of spirit is to our shame, and causes our spiritual life to become impoverished, and to look inwards instead of upwards and outwards. We not only cheat God, but others, by denying Him and them the gift of ourselves. In our thanksgiving after communion we say - "Through your Son Jesus Christ, we offer you our souls and bodies to be a living sacrifice." It is what we call our 'reasonable service', when we consider what God has provided for us and the extent of His love.

In all our dealings with Him and each other, we must adopt the attitude of servants, not demanding or seeking praise, no room for pride, or even expecting a reward. Our Lord spelled out the master/servant relationship - "Would the master thank the servant because he did what he was told to do? So you also, when you have done everything you were told to do, should say - "We are unworthy servants; we have only done our duty." Let us remember Samurai, 'one who serves', and our Lord Jesus who said, "I am among you as one who serves", and give to Him our full allegiance, and whose service is 'perfect freedom'.

The Suffering Community

I do not propose to embark on a discourse on the meaning and purpose of suffering. The question "why?" and "why me?" arises every time we suffer, and can never be fully answered and understood in this life. Here and now we see only a dim shadow of the truth that will one day be revealed. However, we do see in the Word of God some explanation and reason for suffering in the Church. The followers of Jesus suffer along with the rest of humanity through sickness and disease, what others do to us, what we do to ourselves, through so called natural disasters, through circumstances, or events over which we have no control. The suffering which is peculiar to Christians is a direct result of our faith and trust in our Lord Jesus Christ. As we live our lives in obedience to our Lord, we inevitably come into conflict with the world's standards, and the powers of darkness. These are the very forces with which our Lord Himself came into conflict. He came into the world to overthrow and defeat them and and deliver us from their power. This He achieved for us through His death on the cross and His triumphant resurrection. As we identify ourselves with Him and enlist in His army, we identify with His suffering, but we also identify with His victory, and all the spiritual benefits that become ours through Him. The 'Suffering Servant' did not shrink back from the conflict. In total obedience to His Father, He faced it head on, and for our sakes took all the consequences, being obedient even to death on the cross.

Our Lord and Saviour Jesus Christ, through whom all things were made, emptied Himself, and took upon Him the form of a servant, despised and rejected of men, even though He loved them. He did not grasp what He was entitled to; respect, recognition, worship, but allowed Himself to be abused, beaten, and put to death in the cruellest manner devised by man. He forewarned His disciples that they would suffer in the same way, and some were martyred for their faith. He said to them, "If they persecuted me, they will persecute you, and they will do this because they do not know Him who sent me." This has been true for many Christians throughout history, and in modern times under atheistic regimes those who defy the state because of their allegiance to Christ have been imprisoned, tortured and killed. We do not suffer like that in Britain today because we are nominally a Christian country. However, in our private dealings with individuals, socially or in business, we sometimes find ourselves in conflict because of our faith. It is not always easy to confess our belief and trust in Jesus Christ. I am personally aware of having backed down on this on more than one occasion. How often do we rebuke someone who constantly uses the name of Christ as a curse? The Lord says that He will not hold them guiltless who take His name in vain. People should be warned of the consequences of abusing the name that is above all names. This is the name of the one at whose feet every knee shall bow and acknowledge as Lord.

It is easier and safer to identify ourselves with the world, and not stand out as being odd, or worse still, 'religious'. From our baptism we are enlisted as faithful soldiers and servants of Christ, to fight under His banner against sin, the world, and the devil, until our life's end. We make this real and confirm it for ourselves when we are old enough to do so. We can never remain neutral in this battle, but always on active service. This is what is meant by taking up our cross. It is not something which is laid upon us, but which we deliberately and actively do, and we take it up on a daily basis. Our inward self can urge us not to get involved;

it is too risky. But Jesus says, "Whoever would save his life will lose it, and whoever loses his life for my sake, will save it." This is truth and the reality of our condition. As we obey Him, and take up our cross and follow Him, He promises to be with us, and will never allow us to endure more than we are able to bear. We are called to live by faith and not by sight, to trust in the Lord with all our heart, and not rely on our understanding. His promises cannot fail. He cannot deny Himself. Whatever we may be going through at this present time, we know that - "In everything God works together for good to those who love Him, who have been called according to His purpose." - *Romans 8:28*

As we are willing to take up our cross daily, we may face opposition and persecution, even from within the Church. Some may say, "Why all this talk about evangelism. Why force our faith on those who do not want it?" Our Lord's command to His followers was to "go and make disciples of all nations." Spiritual forces of evil will resist this advance into their territory. We go into a suffering world with the message of life and reconciliation, a message of healing and forgiveness, a message of hope and love. That is the message Jesus brought, and that is what His body the Church must do. His reward was suffering and death, and we are called and privileged to share His suffering. But the promise is that if we die with Him, we shall also reign and live with Him. Let us commit ourselves afresh to Him in renewing our baptismal promises, denying ourselves, taking up our cross and following the way of our Saviour and Lord. "The sufferings of this present time are not worth comparing with the glory that is to come." - *Romans 8:18*

The Temple

The Temple; the place where God dwells. What is its significance for us today? In the Acts of the Apostles chapter 7 and verses 44 to 53 we read about the words of Stephen, a man full of God's grace and power who did great wonders and miraculous signs among the people. This was enough to provoke the anger and jealousy among the Jewish religious leaders. Just as they had done with Jesus, they brought false charges against Stephen, had him arrested and brought before the Sanhedrin the Jewish court. Filled with the Holy Spirit, Stephen spoke against these false charges. With a wonderful synopsis of the history of God's dealings with the people of Israel. From Abraham, through the patriarchs, slavery in Egypt, Moses and the exodus, the years in the desert, possession of the promised land under Joshua, times of prosperity under David and Solomon. In his speech before the Sanhedrin, Stephen referred to the Tabernacle in the desert, the tent of meeting, made as God had directed Moses, and where He dwelt with His people. He also spoke about the Temple built by Solomon, and went on to say - "However, the Most High does not live in houses made by men." If this was not enough to provoke further anger, he turned to attack the Jewish leaders, accusing them of resisting the Holy Spirit, of having the same nature as their fathers who persecuted and killed the prophets, even those who predicted the coming of the Messiah. And now, he said - "You have betrayed and murdered Him. You have received the law, but have not obeyed it." For this, Stephen was dragged out of the city and stoned to death. A young man named Saul was there, giving approval to his death.

The Tabernacle was a provisional meeting place of God and His people, the portable sanctuary in which God dwelt with His people in the desert. It was a framed tent of curtains made to a design originated by God through Moses, and contained the ark of the covenant, incense altar, table for the showbread, seven branched candle stick, laver for ritual washing, and the altar of burnt offering. This remained the meeting place beyond the possession of the promised land, right up to the reign of King David. David had built a permanent palace for himself. One day the thought occurred to him - "I dwell in a house of cedar, but the ark of God dwells within curtains." So he collected materials, gathered treasure and bought a site to build a Temple, a house for God. But David was not allowed to build the Temple himself because God said - "You are not to build a house for my Name, because you have shed much blood on earth in my sight. But you will have a son who will be a man of peace. His name will be Solomon. He is the one who will build a house for my Name." The Temple was built in Jerusalem on the site bought by David, and which is now covered by the mosque known as the "Dome of the Rock". It stood for three hundred years, but in 587 BC it was destroyed by Nebuchadnezzar, and the people were taken into exile to Babylon. After the exile, the second Temple was built which stood for five hundred years, and was eventually replaced by Herod's temple commenced in 19 BC. The main structure was finished within ten years and the work continued until 64 AD. It was barely finished before it was destroyed by the Romans in 70 AD.

Jesus greatly respected the Temple, calling it "the house of God." Everything in it was holy because it was sanctified by God who dwelt there, and it was zeal for His Father's house that inspired Him to cleanse it. He said - "My

Father's house shall be a house of prayer, but you have made it a den of robbers." But Jesus said of Himself that "one greater than the Temple is here." It had become a cover for the spiritual barrenness of Israel, and soon it would be destroyed. The accusation produced at His trial asserted that Jesus had taught: "I will destroy this Temple made with hands, and within three days I will build another without hands." The falsity lay in misinterpretation of what Jesus had said. The death of Jesus did in fact result in the supersession of the Temple, and His resurrection put Himself in its place. In the Acts we find the Apostles continuing to worship at the Temple of Jerusalem, but Stephen's defence before the Sanhedrin became an attack on the Temple when he said - "The Most High does not live in houses made by men." God was no longer to be found in the Temple of Jerusalem, but in the hearts of those who are joined to Jesus Christ by faith and are one with Him.

The doctrine of the Church as the realization of the messianic Temple is most prominent in the writings of the Apostle Paul, who as Saul, had approved the death of Stephen. As he says in his letter to the church at Ephesus: "In Jesus the whole building is joined together and rises to become a holy temple in the Lord. And in Him you too are being built together to become a dwelling in which God lives by His Spirit." And to the church at Corinth he says - "don't you know that you are God's temple and that the Holy Spirit lives in you?" This developed further to become our heavenly dwelling, "a building from God, an eternal house in heaven, not built by human hands." In Revelation the vision of the Temple in heaven is not a magnificent edifice but the company of the redeemed, a building which will be completed when the decreed number of the elect is made up. In John's vision he sees that the new Jerusalem has no Temple, but the city itself is cubical like the holy of holies in Solomon's Temple as described in the first Book of Kings. Now John states plainly that God and the Lamb is the Temple. So we see the progression from the Tabernacle, to the Temple, from the Temple to Jesus, from Jesus to His Church, from the Church on earth to the redeemed in heaven, and finally to the New Jerusalem where, in place of the Temple, there is God and His Son. One after another, the barriers separating humankind from God are removed, until nothing remains to hide God from His people. "They will see His face, and His name will be on their foreheads. There will be no more night. They will not need the light of a lamp or the light of the sun, for the Lord will give them light. And they will reign for ever and ever." - *Revelation 22 verses 4 and 5.*

The Upper Room

The disciples of Jesus were assembled together in an upper room on the evening of the first day of the week following the crucifixion of their Lord; and the doors were barred and locked. They were in a state of shock, fear and turmoil. not knowing what to expect. Any moment soldiers might arrive to break down the doors and drag them away for trial and death. But some of the women who had been to the tomb had told them that they had seen the Lord alive, and that He had spoken to them. What were they to make of it? Were the women deluded? Had the tragic events of the last few days turned their minds? Luke records that their words seemed like nonsense to the other disciples, and they did not believe them. Try to imagine the state of tension in that room. All human emotions were there; fear, grief, guilt, depression, disappointment, despair, anger, doubt, hate, love and hope. It was highly charged, volatile, a human time bomb. Fear of death, grief of having deserted their Lord, depression from guilt, disappointment that their hopes had not been realised. "We had hoped that He was the one who was going to redeem Israel." So said two disciples, walking on the road to Emmaus that day. Despair, following dashed hopes; anger, that one of their own friends had betrayed Jesus; doubt concerning the relevance of the last three years; hate towards the Jewish leaders who had perpetrated this crime, and towards the Romans who had brutally executed Him; love for each other in their shared experiences and pain; and some hope that even yet, God would intervene and vindicate them. Perhaps the women were right? Could it be that Jesus was alive? Hadn't He said something about rising after three days?

Then, into that highly charged, locked, barred and shuttered room, the risen Lord Jesus came and stood among them. "Peace be with you", He said. Just as He had stilled the stormy water on the lake with "Peace be still", so He came to calm the troubled waters of their minds and hearts.

There could be no doubt who He was, as He showed them the wounds of crucifixion in His hands, feet and side. "Then they were glad when they saw the Lord." This must be the understatement of all time! The New International Version translates it more appropriately, "overjoyed." The words of a gospel song by Don Francisco picture the scene in his imagination: "Some lifted hands to heaven, and then knelt without a sound; some just stood and stared at Him as if rooted to the ground; but I could not contain the joy that flooded heart and soul; it came rushing out in praises, I had no wish to control – Joy, Joy, Joy!"

But Thomas, who was not with them at the time, would not believe any of them when they told him. He clearly laid down his conditions for belief. Then Jesus came again into that locked room with the same words as before, "Peace be with you", and invited Thomas to see and feel for himself the crucifixion wounds. Thomas could only say in response, "My Lord and my God." What has all this to say to us today? We all put up barriers of one kind or another; against each other; the outside world, and even against God Himself. There can be a locked room within each one of us where we can retreat and feel safe from whatever danger may threaten, whether real or imagined.   But it cuts us off and leaves us isolated. Like all strongholds and fortresses, the security bolts are all on the inside. Fear, grief, guilt, anger, and doubt, can all cause us to do this, like a flower closing up and wilting, and it can rob us of peace and the joy of life.   It may be that for a while, we cannot be reached in that locked room, but there is one for whom locked rooms are no barrier at all. Our Lord Jesus is able to enter into whatever circumstances and problems are causing us to retreat within ourselves. With the eyes of faith, we can see the Son of God who promised, "I am with you always" – "I will never leave you nor forsake you." We see Him there alive, risen from the dead, and see the marks of the nails and the spear. And just as He said to the disciples, so He says to us, "Peace be with you." He knows exactly what we need at any given moment, whether we understand it or not. All our fear, grief, guilt, anger, doubt, was nailed to the cross. He dealt with it there. We died with Him and rose to new life with Him. It is finished. No need to run and hide. Take down the barriers; unlock the doors and come out of the tomb. Even the dead Lazarus came out of the tomb. Jesus can overrule all the conditions we lay down for belief. Light floods into the darkened room, and we can only say with Thomas, "My Lord and my God."

He stands here now among us. Look and see His body broken, and His blood shed for you and me, and rejoice because He lives. He stands among us knowing everything about us; all our hopes and fears; guilt at having let Him down. Whatever our problems, He knows all about them, and He says, "Peace be with you." He's alive and we are forgiven, and we have peace with God and with each other. We come to His table to receive His body and blood, and hear Him say, "Peace I leave with you, my peace I give unto you; do not let your hearts be troubled, neither let them be afraid." As we behold our risen Lord, may joy flood into our hearts and minds, overcoming all other emotions and feelings, just as it did in that upper room two thousand years ago.

The Value of Preaching

I recently heard this humorous definition of a good sermon, "It should have a good beginning and good ending, and the two should be as close together as possible."   Now this makes us laugh, because deep down we recognise that we have some sympathy with this definition. Some sermons can be too long and too boring. But what do you really think of sermons? Do you see them as an opportunity to relax during the service, think about something else, and perhaps have a quiet nap? If so, perhaps you are missing something of vital importance. At best, a sermon can be a message from God Himself. At worst, it can be the airing of personal opinions, without any reference to the Word of God.   I believe that preaching is one of the most privileged activities any human being can be involved with. After all, we boldly declare that we speak in the name of God, Father, Son, and Holy Spirit. What right has anyone to claim that they speak on God's behalf? In fact, only those who believe they are called to do it. "How are they to hear without a preacher, and how can they preach unless they are sent?" *Romans 10:14.* Surely it would be extremely arrogant to speak from the pulpit in one's own name, and expect people to be persuaded to the views of the preacher? I leave you to judge. The preacher is responsible to God for what he or she says in His name, but the hearers also have a responsibility to discern the authentic word of God from that which is false. The prophets of old were chosen by God to go and speak to the people on His behalf. With that authority, and in the power of the Holy Spirit, they were bold to say - "Thus says the Lord." If the people took heed they prospered, but if not, they suffered loss. So it is today. God our Father is always communicating with His Church in various ways, through prayer, reading the word, and through preaching. We suffer loss if we ignore these means of grace. I am an imperfect instrument. Please pray that you will hear the authentic voice of God in these messages.

"We are the body of Christ." We say that every Sunday in our services of the Eucharist. This comes from Romans chapter 12 - "So we, though we are many, are one body in Christ, and individually members one of another." That is a startling statement, and has tremendous implications for us. When we become Christians we become one with Christ, literally part of Him, and one with all other Christians everywhere in the world. We are in him, and He is in us, one with Him for eternity, for He is eternal. That is our privilege, that is our inheritance. There is no greater thought or joy in all the world. We can never again be lonely. He says - "I will never leave you nor forsake you", an eternal promise. All authority has been given to Him, and at His name every knee shall bow. This is the one we worship and adore, and to whom we are joined for evermore! Let this enter into our hearts and minds, and become a living reality. Hold nothing back, give everything you are and have to Him to use for His everlasting praise and glory. What does He require of you? Hear what the Apostle Paul says, "I appeal to you therefore brethren, by the mercies of God, to present your bodies as a living sacrifice, holy and acceptable to God, which is your spiritual worship."

Hannah presented the boy Samuel to Eli in the temple, as she had promised to give him to the Lord, and Samuel became a great prophet. Mary and Joseph brought the baby Jesus to the temple in Jerusalem, and learned from the old man Simeon, who this child was, and what He would do. So we, having been promised to the Lord in our baptism, and confirming the promise for ourselves, are required to present our bodies as a living sacrifice for His use in the world. We lay ourselves on the altar, dead to the world, but alive to God. We come with the gifts that we have received from Him, both our natural and spiritual gifts. The gifts described in Romans 12 are spiritual. No one can prophesy by nature, no one can teach the things of God by nature; they are gifts of the Holy Spirit, which only the children of God can receive. We must recognise the gifts we have, and present them to God to direct and guide how He will use them.

The gifts we have are essential for the proper function of the body of Christ, the Church. Those who are called to full time ministry or other prominent offices, are no more important than those who are called to work unnoticed in the background. The Pharisees were guilty of pride when they liked to be seen in public places and greeted as 'Rabbi'. That is why Paul bids us not to think more highly of ourselves than we aught to think, but to think with sober judgment. Having gifts that differ, we must use them. Sometimes God puts us in situations where we are called upon to do things of which we never dreamed we were capable, and our spiritual gift becomes apparent. The old priest Simeon, held the baby Jesus in his arms and called Him "a light to lighten the Gentiles." We are called to bear that light and carry it to others, that they too may see and believe. We share that privilege together as one body in Christ. Let us then highly value one another, sharing and using our gifts; walking in love and peace with each other, and working together as one body. Let us consider before God, where we belong in this body, how we can present ourselves as a living sacrifice to His praise and glory, and the extension of His kingdom here on earth.

The Wedding at Cana

I suppose that most of us enjoy an occasional glass of wine, and some perhaps even more than an occasional glass, especially at times of celebration such as at Christmas, New Tear and Birthday Parties. There is nothing wrong with that, provided that we remain in control of the quantity consumed, and therefore in control of ourselves. Wine production is a vast industry, and is much talked about and written about. Many people make their own wine out of anything from grapes to any vegetable or fruit that grows in their gardens. In the Bible there are many references, both in the Old and New Testaments, to wine and vines and vineyards. Wine and corn together stand for a full and adequate supply of food and of good gifts of life. Isaac's blessing on Jacob included these words – "May God give you the heaven's dew and of earth's richness – an abundance of grain and new wine." So, wine is one of God's good gifts to be enjoyed, but there are dangers, and the Bible contains warnings about its misuse. The abuse of alcohol is, and always has been, a cause of terrible suffering in the world. Used symbolically, the vine was the emblem of prosperity and peace among the ancient Hebrews. More particularly, it symbolized the chosen people. They were the vine that God had taken out of slavery in Egypt, and had planted in a choice land "flowing with milk and honey". They had been given all the attention necessary for the production of outstanding fruit, but instead had yielded only wild grapes. In the New Testament, no fewer than five parables relate to vines and their culture. Particularly significant is our Lord's description of Himself as the True Vine, with all believers as branches producing fruit as they remain connected to the source of all life and blessing.

In the Gospel of John chapter 2, we read about a celebration at which wine was consumed, and at which Jesus was present. The wedding at Cana is a well known story in which a wonderful miracle occurred, the changing of water into wine. Jesus, His mother, and His disciples had been invited to the wedding, and they were all there. Jesus did not disdain from being present at a social event where alcohol was consumed, and no doubt, over indulged by some of the guests. It was the custom to bring out the best wine first, and then the cheaper wine after the guests had reached the point where they would not be able to discriminate! It is the recurring nightmare of hosts that there won't be enough food and drink for their guests; which is why there is always more than enough at church pooled suppers! But here, on this occasion, the unthinkable had happened, to the shame and embarrassment of the master of the banquet. They had run out of wine! So Mary told Jesus – "They have no more wine." She brought the problem to the one who could solve it and clearly expected Him to do something, because she said to the servants – "do whatever He tells you." Most people are surprised at the apparent rough way Jesus replies to His mother, which in the Authorized Version reads – "woman, what have I to do with you? My hour has not yet come." In the New International Version, it is softened to read – "Dear woman, why do you involve me? …. My time has not yet come." However, the servants did what He told them, filled the six large jars, used for ceremonial washing, with water. They drew out some, which had now become wine, and took it to the master of the banquet, who was amazed at the quality of the wine. Contrary to custom, the best wine had been saved till last.

Apart from being a demonstration of God's power over created things, what else can we learn from these events? This is the first of the miracles recorded by John, which he refers to as 'signs' in which God's glory is revealed. On this occasion of a wedding feast we see God's intimate involvement with human social life, including His compassion for the results of human failure and lack of foresight, poor planning. We learn something about intercession, in being privileged to bring concern for others to His attention. Not telling Him what to do, but to rest in the knowledge that in His own time and ways He will act in response to our petitions. As His servants, we learn that if we do what whatever He tells us, the result will be the very best for us and for others. We must learn to recognise and obey His commands. As we do this, wonderful things will happen which will be signs to unbelievers, when they see what God has done, and will put their faith in Him. Above all, we learn the greater nature of the new covenant over the old. The water used for ceremonial washing rituals can never cleanse moral defilement, but the blood of Jesus purifies us from all sin. It is as we come to celebrate the Eucharist, that we have the opportunity to consider the meaning and value of the communion wine, the precious blood of our Lord and Saviour Jesus Christ, poured out for us, and by which alone, we are made clean from all that defiles and degrades us.

Wedding at Cana

The Work of Disciples

What is a disciple?   The word is from the Latin meaning a pupil or learner. Greek philosophers and Jewish Rabbis gathered round them groups of apprentices or learners.   John the Baptist, and our Lord Jesus Himself, did the same. Disciples are those who accept the teaching of others, and so Christian disciples accept the teaching of Jesus, and confess Him as the Christ. There follows, three aspects of Christian discipleship:

1. Disciples in relation to God.
2. In relation to other disciples.
3. In relation to the world.

<u>Disciples in relation to God.</u> The first thing we see is that we are called to be disciples. We do not choose God; He chooses us. That is not to say that we have no free will in the matter. We can choose to say no! Through His Son, God says, "Follow me", but it is a free will decision of ours to do so, to respond to the call. The second thing we see is that we are called individually, and in various ways according to our own particular needs, personality and circumstances. The third thing we see is that we are meant to be dependant on our God for everything we need. We acknowledge His omnipotence and our weakness, and learn to trust Him at all times. Then we see that He has work for us to do, and that He provides the spiritual gifts and the power to do His will in the world, to bring about His purposes. No doubt He could do it without us, but in His infinite love and wisdom, He has chosen to involve us in the work of extending His kingdom, to be co-workers with Him. Lastly, we see that He has chosen us to be with Him forever, to share in His eternal kingdom, to inherit all that He has for us in His Son. Who would not want

to be the disciple of a Master like that? Is there any greater privilege or joy on earth to compare with it?

<u>Disciples in relation to other disciples.</u> Just as natural birth brings us into a family where we grow and learn, so spiritual birth brings us into the family of the Church, where we grow and learn in fellowship with brothers and sisters in Christ. And just as we do not choose our natural family, so we do not choose our spiritual family. Personalities and temperaments will inevitably cause friction and tension, but we are called to love one another. We are called to support and comfort each other, and to share what we have, our gifts, wealth, our experiences of God. We are meant to see the infinite worth of fellow disciples. Whether we accept them or not, God has accepted them. We are meant to recognize disciples outside our own particular denomination, persuasion or tradition.

Christian fellowship breaks down where one particular party is convinced it has received all the truth, and has nothing to learn from anyone else. Such arrogance is to be deplored. God cannot be pigeon-holed into watertight compartments. That is not to say that we should tolerate that which clearly contradicts the Word of God, but we must be open to the truth others have received, which we have not. We are told to test the spirits to see if they are of God, but it is only by the Holy Spirit that we can do this, as we allow Him to fill us with the truth as it is revealed in Jesus. Lastly, we see that we are called to increase our fellowship, to be fruitful and multiply, to bring others into the family of God.

Disciples in relation to the world. The conversion of the Pharisee, Saul of Tarsus, on the road to Damascus must surely be the most amazing and dramatic U-turn in the the whole of human history, with far reaching consequences for the world. Here was a man full of knowledge concerning the Law, steeped in the traditions of the fathers, and full of zeal in his determination to put down this new sect which appeared to threaten Judaism. When Jesus spoke to him on the road, Saul's response was, "Who are you Lord?" It seems he already knew in his heart who it was. He had witnessed and consented to the death by stoning of Stephen, the first Christian martyr. This was his commission from Jesus to the Gentiles - "I send you to open their eyes, and turn them from darkness to light, from the dominion of Satan to God, so that, by trust in me, they may obtain forgiveness of sins, and a place with those whom God has made His own." The essential work of Christian disciples is to make more disciples. This is not the special activity of the few, but the glorious privilege of the whole people of God. Perhaps this can be remembered by this short summary of the three aspects of discipleship as they relate to the clear commands of Jesus:

Disciples in relation to God, "Do this in remembrance of me."
Disciples in relation to other disciples, "Love one another."
Disciples in relation to the world, "Go and make disciples of all nations."

Those in Authority

From the very beginning when God created humankind in His own image, He gave them authority over the whole earth and everything in it - "Be fruitful and increase in number; fill the earth and subdue it." *Genesis 1 verse 28.* This authority brought with it responsibility, and ultimately humankind would be called to give account to their Creator for what they had done with what they had been given. The Fall brought with it corruption in the whole of creation, and its whole history shows God's plan to bring about restoration and reconciliation, and complete His ultimate intention for the world.

I want to focus on two individual characters in Scripture who were both in positions of authority over others. These are King Belshazzar, son of Nebuchadnezzar, and ruler of the Babylonian empire around 550BC; and Porcius Festus, the Roman governor of Judea, 59 to 62 AD. Nebuchadnezzar had exalted himself above Israel's God, but had been humbled and finally brought to confession of his sin. His son, Belshazzar, had not learned from his father's experience, and continued in blasphemy and idolatry, and without repentance. His final blasphemy was a great banquet when he and his nobles and concubines drank wine from the gold and silver goblets taken from the Temple of God in Jerusalem. As they drank, they praised the gods of gold and silver, of bronze, iron, wood and stone. It was judgment time for Belshazzar, and he was terrified when he saw the hand writing on the plaster of the palace wall. The writing was literally on the wall for him, and this is where, in chapter 5 of the Book of Daniel, this expression comes from. Belshazzar had abused the power and authority given to him by God to a point where there was no possibility of repentance, and inevitable judgment followed. Porcius Festus had the authority of the great Roman empire behind him as the governor of Judea. But like Pontius Pilate before him, was more concerned with having an easy life than he was with fairness and justice. It was within his power to release the Apostle Paul on charges brought against him by the Jews. As he said himself - "I found that he had done nothing deserving of death." But wishing to do the Jews a favour, he found an excuse to pass the case to a higher authority, and thus rid himself of a little local problem.

If people are appointed by God to positions of authority, or at least allowed by Him to obtain power, we may wonder why so many of them commit such evil acts. We think of such monsters as Adolf Hitler, Idi Amin, or Pol Pot. It has been said that power corrupts, and that appears to be true where there is no effective democratic control. The fact is that we all have responsibility towards God for the things we do, or fail to do. People in authority are placed there mainly to maintain law and order and to execute justice, to create a society in which everyone can achieve their maximum potential.   That is the ideal, but because we are all flawed by sin, it is not realised. People fail and abuse their authority when they do not acknowledge that they have such a responsibility towards God and their fellow men, and seek to exploit their position for their own personal gain. Christians should not behave in such a manner because they should be aware with the psalmist - "O Lord, you have searched me and you know me. You know when I sit down and when I rise; you perceive my thoughts from afar. You discern my going out and my lying down; you are familiar with all my ways. Before a word is on my tongue you know it completely, O Lord." - *Psalm 139 verses 1 to 4.* In any *case,* Christians should serve God with the bonds of love and not compulsion. Those entrusted with power will be judged according to what they have been given. The justice of God is this - "From everyone to whom much has been given, much will be required."- *Luke 12 verse 48.* There is the power which comes from wealth, and this is very much sought after today, and which can become a snare and deception if not handled responsibly. Those in authority, unless they recognise a greater power outside of themselves, are in great danger of yielding to temptation and corruption.   It is not surprising that Christians are called upon to pray for all in authority. The Apostle Paul, in his first letter to Timothy, with instructions on worship, says - "I urge you, then, first of all, that requests, prayers, intercession and thanksgiving be made for everyone; for kings and all those in authority, that we may live peaceful and quiet lives in all godliness and holiness." - *1 Timothy 2 verse 1.*

Power corrupts because humankind is by nature corruptible. Fortunately, final power does not rest with us, but with God who has given all authority to His Son. Just before His ascension into heaven, Jesus told His disciples - "All authority in heaven and on earth has been given to me." He promised to be with them always. What a great comfort it is to know that we are not ultimately in the hands of corruptible humankind, but a loving Father whose ways are just and whose judgments are true. The dream of the songwriter who wrote "If I ruled the world", would in fact be a nightmare if actually realised!   Recognising responsibility for our own areas of authority and ministry, let us reflect and meditate on the lovely prayer by King David in *Psalm 139 verses 23 and 24* - "Search me, O God, and know my heart; test me and know my anxious thoughts. See if there is any offensive way in me, and lead me in the way everlasting."

True Healing

Doctors are rarely mentioned in the Bible, and where they are, they do not appear to merit any degree of success. For example, Mark tells us that the woman with the flow of blood had suffered at the hands of doctors for many years, and had spent all she had. But instead of getting better, she grew worse. The Jews had their own sanitary laws given by God, and which seem to have spared them many of the diseases suffered by other nation states. Today, especially in our western civilisation, and in spite of the problems facing our own NHS, medical practitioners are generally highly regarded for their diagnostic skills and treatment for sickness, aided by modern technology, especially in surgical operations. Simple operations can save the and restore the sight of thousands in Africa. The provision of clean pure water for drinking, cooking and irrigation, can transform a community back to health. But the Church still has an important role in the healing process, which is recognised by the medical profession as part of holistic medicine, where the mind and spirit are seen as vital in promoting wholeness. In remembering the work of doctors, surgeons, nurses, modern medicine and technology in the relief of pain and suffering, we must not forget there is a deeper need of spiritual healing which is the ministry of the Church. Today, we do not expect to see miraculous healing events as recorded in the days of Jesus and the Apostles, and yet we are still encouraged to pray for the sick and to expect God to act in response to our prayers of faith, as evidenced by wholeness and healing services.

In the 5th chapter of the letter of James verses 13 to 16 we see all the ingredients involved in a service of healing. Songs of praise, elders of the church, faith, prayer, anointing with oil, and confession in the form of sharing problems with another person. Analogies are sometimes helpful if not taken to extremes. In thinking about ingredients our minds inevitably turn to the subject of food and preparation of meals. To have the right ingredients is one thing, but to produce a wholesome nourishing dish requires an expert cook or chef, good preparation, balance and timing, careful blending and attractive presentation. All food is provided by God to promote health, enjoyment and growth.

Our songs of praise are the hymns we sing. The elders are the ordained and lay ministers who lead the service. Faith is evidenced in the fact of our presence here, a recognition of our need and the only source of true healing. Prayer is the essence of what we are doing, and without which no healing would be possible. The anointing oil was a medical remedy in New Testament times, as well as a symbol of God's powerful presence. Sharing problems promotes the healing process. We are weak and fallible human beings, and our best endeavours do not always produce the ideal conditions for healing. The prayers of the elders and the people are essential in all aspects of the service, acknowledging our weakness and seeking the guidance and strength of God through the Holy Spirit. We all need to believe in the power of God to heal, and His desire to do so, while acknowledging that all healing comes from Him and only in accordance with His will and purpose for our lives. Faith in God should not be lost because a sick person is not healed, or at least not in the way we expect. Prayer is never a device by which God can be manipulated into doing my will. Faithful disciples accept God's answer to prayer whatever it may be. But prayer has great power in the ministry of the

Church to the sick, and we can be encouraged in all its forms. God may relieve the suffering, but as the Apostle Paul found with his 'thorn in the flesh', God's grace was sufficient for him.

Let us be assured and encouraged as we come in faith before God our Father and Creator, with our problems, pains, cares and sickness, that we have come to the source of true healing. In His infinite wisdom and love, He will give us what we need and not necessarily what we want or expect. In our human limitation we only see short term remedies, but He knows the long term eternal remedy for all our ills, and which will only be finally resolved when our Lord and Saviour, Jesus Christ, returns as King and Judge. Then as we read in the *Revelation to John chapter 21 verse 3* - "God Himself will be with His people and He will wipe away every tear from their eyes. There will be no more death or mourning or crying or pain, for the old order of things has passed away." In the meantime, let us take advantage of the means of healing that our Father has provided through services of healing, and praise Him for His infinite love, goodness and mercy.

Vision of God's Church

This church has a vision of growing as people discover their need of Jesus Christ, and experience love and care in its fellowship. The key words are - growing, love, care and fellowship. The Church can grow in two ways, upwards and outwards. Upwards in the sense of growing into spiritual maturity, and outwards by expanding, being fruitful and multiplying. To grow up is to become adult, to gain wisdom and knowledge through experience. As we grow upwards we are more likely to grow outwards. To love one another is a clear direct command of our Lord to His disciples, and one which He repeated several times. It is not an optional extra, but essential if we are to grow both upwards and outwards. It is the clear sign to the world that we are His disciples if we love one another. Care can be described as love in action, and the fellowship we have is of the Holy Spirit, because, "by one Spirit we were all baptised into one body." We are the body of Christ. In his first letter to the church in Corinth, chapter 12, the Apostle Paul uses the analogy of the human body to describe how the Church works - "Christ is like a single body which has many parts; it is still one body even though it is made up of different parts." The human body is very vulnerable to accident and disease. I once suffered severe back pain, and was disabled for about one month, hardly able to move. Is the Church disabled, or is everything as it should be? We are full of admiration for world class athletes, but what they have achieved is by hard training, commitment, determination, self control, pain and suffering, with a clear aim of being the best in the world.

When I was conscripted into the army for National Service at age 18, after basic training, I was stationed in Singapore as a draughtsman in the Royal Engineers

Regiment. For reasons which I can no longer recall, I found myself in the regimental tug-of-war team. Our trainer was the Regimental Sergeant Major who rigged up a huge tripod with pulley wheels and a large box full of concrete and railway wheels. We were trained by pulling this box up and down as a team and individually, and not allowed to stop until we were told to, or near collapse! The end result of all this was that we were unbeatable, and our proudest moment was in winning the Far East Land Forces Tournament against the Royal Marine Commandos. The point of this is that apart from the hard training, our success depended on working together, digging in, holding and pulling together as one. It was tough but the reward was great. The human body works at maximum efficiency when all its parts are healthy and working together in harmony and co-operation, controlled by a healthy dedicated mind.

As members of the body of Christ, the Church, it is our individual responsibility to find our proper place in the body, and to be content in the role. Using our spiritual gifts, we commit ourselves wholeheartedly to that task for the benefit of the whole. The Holy Spirit was very much in control in the early Church, and wonderful things happened. Our effectiveness is in direct proportion to our openness to the Holy Spirit and our willingness to be obedient to His leading. It is availability which is vital, not our ability. But it is part of our freedom to say no to God. We can say at any stage, thus far and no further. We create the barriers and put up the road blocks by our unwillingness and unbelief. We still find in ourselves that tendency to want to retain some control and not let go completely, fearful of what that could mean. Matthew tells us that when our Lord visited his own country

He did not do many mighty works there because of their unbelief. Is our unbelief preventing Him from doing mighty works here? We may feel safer as we are, so we put it off. Our potential has not been realised. The word potent means powerful.   The body of Christ, the Church, is the most powerful thing on earth if it realises its potential. It can only do that by faith, believing and acting on the promises of God. The first Christians did, and they turned the world upside down. If we are true to our vision and pursue it, wherever it leads, then we shall see mighty works as our Father shows is power and love to a hungry and thirsty world.

Wisdom

This is what the Apostle James tells us about the need for wisdom - "If any of you lacks wisdom, let him ask God who gives to everyone generously and without reproaching, and it will be given him. But let him ask in faith, with no doubting." - *James 1 verse 5*

So what is wisdom, how can we define it? It is the ability, or result of an ability, to think and act using knowledge, experience, understanding, common sense and insight. It is the art of being successful, of forming the correct plan to gain the desired results, and its seat is the heart, the centre of moral and intellectual decision. That is all very well, but what about Christian wisdom? How does it differ, if at all, from worldly wisdom? Of course they have much in common, because of our common humanity. Even wisdom derived from natural abilities or distilled from experience, is a gracious gift, because God's creative activity makes such wisdom possible. But in Psalm 111 verse 10, and in Proverbs chapter 1 verse 7, we read that - "The fear of the Lord is the beginning of wisdom." In Proverbs there are over fifty references to wisdom. Such wisdom takes insights gleaned from the knowledge of God's ways, and applies them in the daily walk. Insight in itself is not enough. It must be applied practically to be of any use to individuals and communities. Pagan wisdom has no anchor in the covenant God, and is therefore doomed to failure. As the Scripture says - "Woe unto them that are wise in their own eyes." Worldly wisdom is based on intuition and experience without revelation. But the truly wise are those to whom God has graciously imparted wisdom. Such a wise person was King Solomon. He was humble enough to acknowledge that he was totally inadequate in himself to govern the people, to discern between good and evil. When the Lord appeared to him in a dream at night, God said to him: "Ask what I shall give you." Solomon replied: "Give your servant an understanding mind to govern your people." The wisdom of Solomon is legendary, and to him is attributed much of the Book of Proverbs, the Song of Songs and Ecclesiastes. His reign in Israel was the most glorious, prosperous and relatively peaceful periods in the history of the Jewish nation.

How does all this apply to us? Wisdom in the fullest sense belongs to God, and therefore wisdom as it applies to humans is relative and limited to the purposes for which God created individuals to serve Him in His Church, and witness to His love, power and glory, in their community. People who are called to positions of power and authority in society, are in special need of wisdom. Their Christian faith doesn't necessarily mean that they will always make wise or moral decisions. But we need to pray for them in their positions of great responsibility for the sake of peace and security. But what about relatively insignificant individual Christians and our corporate church life? We certainly need wisdom in respect of various problems in the Church. Problems which tend to dominate the news and obscure the primary task of the Church to preach the gospel in word and action. People are turning more to meditational therapies such as yoga, tai chi and feng shui, looking for answers within themselves. Sadly, the Church itself has been an instrument of dissatisfaction and disaffection among seekers after spiritual truth, with peripheral disputes, liberal theology, and a gospel diluted with human philosophy instead of being the instrument of proclamation and revelation by which our Lord Jesus Christ can be recognised and acknowledged as the

Saviour of the world. It is immeasurably tragic that in rejecting the Church, people are seen to be rejecting the Lord of life, the one to whom everyone must one day give account. For everyone of us must appear before the judgment of Christ to receive what has been done in the body, whether good or bad.

The Apostle Paul, in his letter to the church at Ephesus, chapter 1 verse 7, says: "I keep asking that the God of our Lord Jesus Christ, the glorious Father, may give you the Spirit of wisdom and revelation, so that you may know Him better." What more incentive could we have than to know God better? We need to pray specifically for wisdom in each situation where we find our own resources inadequate, just as Solomon did, to find our rightful place in God's Church, to be the people He created us to be, and to reveal and share with others all the good things our loving Father has given us in His Son. Let us therefore continue to pray to our God for wisdom, "who gives to everyone generously and without reproaching, and it will be given him. But let him ask in faith with no doubting."

Words, Words, Words

As a licensed Reader I have been conscious of the need to pray for spiritual wisdom in the awesome responsibility of speaking in the name of God, the Creator of the universe! It is a great source of comfort for any preacher to trust in the promise of God, through the prophet Isaiah, that His word will not return to Him empty, but will accomplish what He desires, and will succeed in the purpose for which He sent it. - *Isaiah 55 verse 11*

"Words, words, words! I'm so sick of words", said Eliza Doolittle in the musical 'My Fair Lady'. But what would we do without words? For a start we would be less than human, because it is the gift of language that makes us uniquely different from the rest of God's creatures. Through language our Creator can communicate with us, and we can respond to Him. It is our ability to communicate with words, the exchange of information, ideas and feelings, which gives us power and authority over the rest of creation. What we have done with such power and authority is another question, and one that the Christian faith tries to deal with, because words can be used for good or evil, to build up or destroy, to speak truth or lies. In our Anglican liturgy we say "this is the Word of the Lord" after every Bible reading, when we can reflect on what it means to us as a worshipping and witnessing community. I want to focus attention on three aspects of the Word of the Lord; the spoken word, the written word, and the living word.

We communicate, most directly and intimately, by speech, either face to face, or from a distance by telephone or by whatever sophisticated technology is available. We understand that it was by the spoken word that God commanded the creation of the universe. In the beginning God created the heavens and the earth. God said - "Let there be light', and there was light. He spoke and it was done, and so it was for the rest of His creative acts, culminating in the creation of humankind. Then God said - "let us make humankind in our image, in our likeness." It was by the spoken word that God communicated His laws to fallen humanity which had become estranged from Him. It was through the prophets that God spoke to His people Israel, so that they were able to say - "this is what the Lord says." The Apostle Peter says - "No prophecy recorded in Scripture was thought up by the prophet himself. It was the Holy Spirit within these godly men who gave them the true messages from God."   It was through the prophets that God communicated His plan of forgiveness and reconciliation; incompletely through the shedding of blood of sacrificial lambs, but ultimately, supremely and completely, through the precious blood of Christ, the Lamb of God who takes away the sins of the world. In this paraphrased version from the Living Bible, the prophet Isaiah foretells the crucifixion of Jesus - "He was oppressed and afflicted, yet He never said a word. He was brought as a lamb to the slaughter; and as a sheep before her shearers is dumb, so He stood silent before the ones condemning Him. From prison and trial, they led Him away to His death. But who among the people of that day realised it was their sins He was dying for; that He was suffering their punishment? He was buried like a criminal in a rich man's grave; but He had done no wrong, and had never spoken an evil word."

What the prophets said was recorded on parchment scrolls, and the spoken word became the written word which has been handed down to us today. The written word is a powerful medium. There seems to be no end to the number of books written on every subject under the sun, and now on the internet, we are able to tap into whatever information is available. The ministry of Jesus was very short; about three years from His baptism in the River Jordan to His death and resurrection. The four Gospels are an essential, but not complete, record of everything that Jesus said and did. The Apostle John says that if all the other events in the life of Jesus were written, the whole world could not contain the books.

As well as the spoken word and the written word, there is another way we can communicate, and that is by the living word which is what we are and what we do, and very often speaks louder than what we say. Actions speak louder than words, we say. The writer of the letter to the Hebrews says - "In the past God spoke to our forefathers through the prophets at many times and in many ways, but in these last days He has spoken to us by His Son, whom He appointed heir of all things, and through whom He made the universe." This is the Word who was with God and who was God, our Lord Jesus Christ who became flesh and dwelt among us. In Him we see the one in whom all spoken and written words become a reality, the living Word. As He said - "If you have seen me, you have seen the Father; I and the Father are one." Jesus is the living expression of all that God is; His very nature.

As worshipping Christians, we celebrate the Eucharist. This is what we also call the Communion which has the same meaning as communication. God communicates with us, shows His love for us, in the symbols of the body and blood of Christ, the bread and the wine, which we share in common. We are in communion with God and with each other in a deep and meaningful way. We hear the voice of Jesus saying: "This is my body broken for you; this is my blood poured out for you." We give thanks for the spoken word, the written word, and especially for the living Word, our Lord Jesus Christ who has returned to the Father. As the living Word He has not returned empty, but has accomplished the Father's desire, and succeeded in the purpose for which He was sent. Now we look for His coming again in glory. Not in poverty and obscurity, but as King and Judge, and everyone will see Him, and in every language confess that Jesus Christ is Lord, to the glory of God the Father.

Poems

Rhyme and Reason

Big Bang

In the Beginning
There was a Big Bang
That simply explains
How it all began.

Some matter exploded
Began to expand
Created the universe
Created the land

Nothing before that
As far as we know
Till thirteen
Billion years ago?

And Big Bang said
Let there be light
And so it was
Light and bright

Light brought life
And life was good
Then on the earth
The first humans stood

A mystery to science
Till Darwin's solution
Complete explanation
It's called evolution

It starts with a bang
Evolves to perfection
But how to explain
Its persistent infection

It can't have a purpose
For that means a 'God'
And that's just a cop out
A wallop of cod

Life's without meaning
A pointless endeavour
All comes to an end
Won't go on forever

Where's perfect justice
It just isn't there
So what is the point
To try to be fair

No God no judgment
The question is fraught
So do what you like
It all comes to naught

Love's a great mystery
No science can explain
It comes from Big Bang
Like evil and pain

All who have faith
In Jesus the Word
Know He is the Truth
He is the Lord

He came to this earth
To recover our loss
Took our sins on Himself
On Calvary's cross

Secured our forgiveness
And so made us good
Reserved us for heaven
Saved by His blood

Take heart Christian people
Away with your fears
What starts with Big Bang
Won't end in tears

Big Bang

Big Brother

Big Brother
Is watching you
George Orwell says
In his book
Nineteen Eighty-Four

We are watched
By surveillance
And speed cameras
Because we can't be
Trusted to behave

More and more
Control by the State
More legislation
Restricting our freedom
To do good or evil

Where will it end
Nobody knows
Identity cards
Nothing hidden
From the law

Big Brother
Is oppressive
Brought about
By fear and to
Control lawlessness

There is another
Big Brother
Who is not
Oppressive but
Loving and caring

He watches us
Not to control
But to guide
And lead us
Into righteousness

He is Lord
Of all creation
And who died to
Give us life in
All its fullness

This Big Brother
Is not to be feared
But to be adored
And followed
Into eternal life

Let us not hide
From this one who
Watches us but
Trust in his love
And mercy always

Big Brother

Christmas Jingle

Beneath the tinsel and flashing lights
Jingle bells the reindeer sleigh
The Child lies buried
Suffocated by sentiment
Crucified by Christmas

But see Him rise and ascend
In the hearts of the faithful
Who have not forgotten
That He is our Friend
Who died for our redemption

Summoned by angels led by a star
The poor and the wise
Came to the stable
To present their gifts
To the infant King

One day all must come
To lay their gifts at His feet
To worship Him as Lord and King
For that is who He is
Through time and in eternity

Sing choirs of angels
Sing in exultation
Sing all you citizens
Of heaven above
Glory to God in the highest
O come let us adore Him
Christ the Lord

Christmas Jingle

Gloucester Cathedral

Stone upon stone to the glory of God
With unbelievable skill and patience
The masterpiece was constructed
How many years and lives
Were willingly devoted to it
Now it stands proclaiming
The more noble aspirations of man
Using the creative skills bestowed
By the faithful Creator
To provide a fitting place
In which to worship Him

On a sunny afternoon in May
All is peace without and within
Inside it is cool and the sunlight
Filters through the stained glass
The German party sits quietly enthralled
As the student guide describes the vaulting
But outside the Polish couple from Oxford
Talk about the disturbing city
What do they mean
They mean the drug addicts
And drunks in the city square

How can man construct such beauty
And be the instrument of self destruction
In the shadow of the cathedral
Is the shadow of death
Tares have been sown among the wheat
But the One whose name
Is carved in stone says
I have come that they might have life,
And life in all its abundance
Let us go out into the heat of the day
And call them in to the cool shelter of Christ

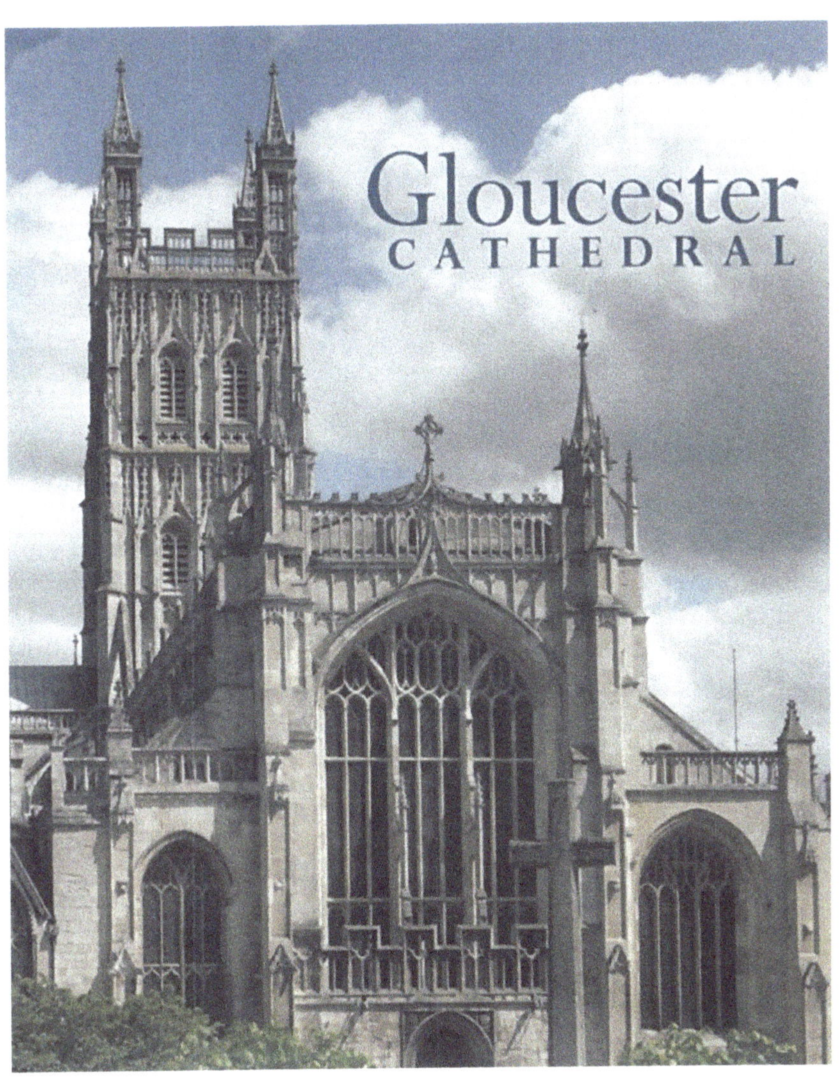

Gloucester
CATHEDRAL

It Stands to Reason

It stands to reason
What we inherit
Is handed down
What was theirs
Becomes our own

It stands to reason
We inherit gifts
That are not owed
Natural gifts in
Our genetic code

It stands to reason
We are part of what
Our parents were
Isn't he like him
Isn't she like her

It stands to reason
Our very natures
Are handed on
From generation
To generation

It stands to reason
A perfect man
Could not be
Begot by a sinner
Like you or me

It stands to reason
Jesus the Christ
Was not begot
By Mary's husband
If not..... then what

It stands to reason
Said the angel to Mary
You will bear a son
Name him Jesus
Son of God Holy One

It stands to reason
Jesus born of Mary
To bless the human race
Begot by the Holy Spirit
Full of truth and grace

It Stands to Reason

Song of Songs

All the love songs
Ever written
Become a reality
In Christ

I will love
You forever
Has no meaning
Apart from Him

His love
Is eternal
It does not fade
Or grow dim

He is hurt
By indifference
Deeply wounded
By unfaithfulness

But He will
Never leave us
He will never
Stop loving us

His promise
Is unbreakable
He cannot
Deny what He is

He looks for
Our response
Of love
For Him

All the love songs
Ever written
Become a reality
In Christ

Song of Songs

The Empty Words Psalm

The Deceiver is my leader
Why should I doubt
He explains facts of science
But gives hope in nothing
He despises my soul

He leads me in the paths
Of delusion for his own sake
When I walk through the valley
Of the shadow of death
There is no helper

For no one is with me
To protect me
No one to guide me
To give me peace
And comfort me

He prepares a fable (sic)
Before me to the delight
Of the scoffers
He anoints my faith with soil
And tramples religion underfoot

Surely all deceivers
Shall bother me
All the days of my life
And I will live with the voice
Of the far too clever.

Ahem

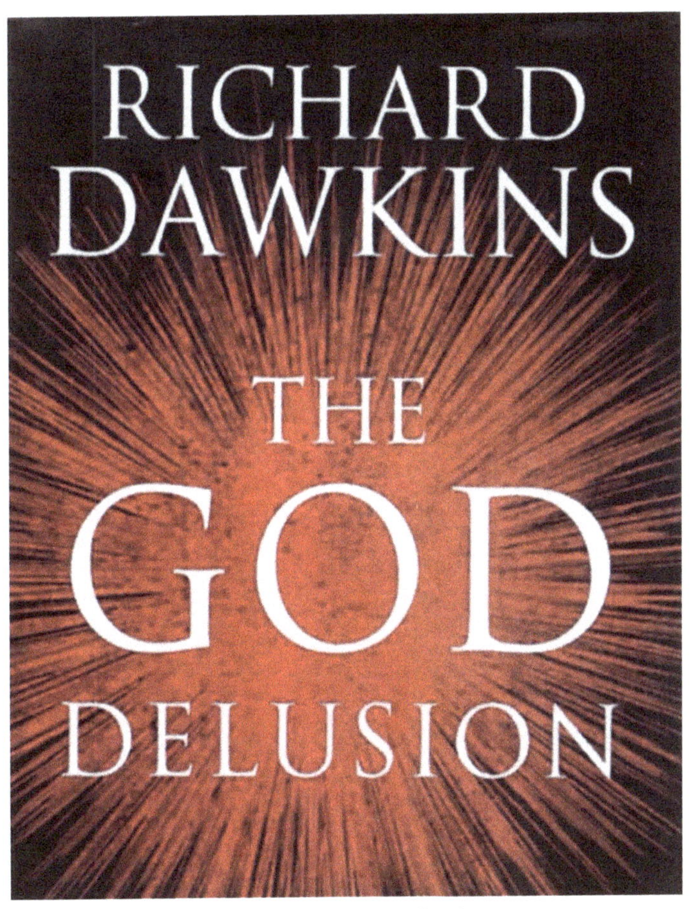

The Empty Words Psalm

What is Love

What is love
How can you describe it
Something everyone needs
For health and wholeness

Not something
Prescribed by a doctor
Not something traded
Over the shop counter

Love is precious
Much to be desired
More valuable than
All the world's gold
People without love
Are badly damaged
With distorted
Views of the world

Like fruit dried up
And shrivelled
On the trees of
Neglect and indifference
But love pours in
The sun and the rain
To yield a harvest
Of fruitful abundance

Where hate destroys
Love builds up
Promotes peace
Warms the heart
Love is Jesus
Praying three times
In the garden
Sweat falling like blood

Father let this cup
Pass from me
Yet not my will
But your will be done
Love is the betrayal
The arrest the desertion
And the trial
The brutal scourging

Love is the Crucifixion
The torn flesh
The twisted body

We sin because
We are sinners
But from the foot

Of the Cross look up
The blood deals with
What we have done
The Cross deals with
What we are

The precious blood
Of Jesus
Cleanses me
From all sin
I have been crucified
With Christ
It is no longer I who live
But Christ who lives in me

Love reaches down
To the depths
Of our despair
And desolation
It lifts us up
To sit forever
With Christ
In the heavenly realms

Love is good news
Of resurrection
New life
In Christ
Freely offered
To all who
Will receive it
By faith

Love is sharing
The good news
With all who
Live in darkness
Superstition
And loneliness
Without hope
In the world

Love is forgiveness
Love is reconciliation
Love is communication

The blood poured out
Love is the shame
The nakedness
The cry of desolation
Why have you forsaken me

Love is eternal
Love is the Cross
Love is Jesus
Jesus is God
GOD IS LOVE

217

What is Love

ALLEGORIES

Sea of Life - Allegory

I invite you to come with me in your imagination, on a warm sunny afternoon, to stand on the cliffs looking out beyond a golden beach, to the restless sea called the 'Sea of Life'. Suddenly a great fleet of tall ships appears. The ships of various shapes and sizes with their white sails unfurled, are making good progress with a following wind, all heading in the same direction but on slightly different courses. What a magnificent sight! As we focus our binoculars on the fleet we see that they all have the same type of flag at their mast head. Its design is cruciform; a white cross on a black background, and is called the 'Captain's Banner'. Just below it there is another flag with a different design for each ship. We focus on one particular ship and see that its special flag has a red cross on a white background. It is called 'The Ensign of St. George', and the name on the bow is 'SS Church of England'. In our privileged position we are allowed in our imagination to come aboard. The first thing we notice is that this is not a passenger ship, because all the people on board are working crew, with different jobs to do. The officers all have uniforms, and those on the upper decks have the most magnificent ones, and carry out more ceremonial duties than the ones on the lower decks. The crew on the middle decks appear to be very busy, and the ones on the lower decks are dressed in boiler suits, and don't seem to have much time for ceremonial duties. None of them seem to be aware that hidden away out of sight there are some stowaways on board, just there for the ride, and not quite sure where they are going. There is one important ceremony they all share. When the invitation comes to 'splice the main-brace', they meet together and eat a small ship's biscuit and drink from a silver cup of red wine. This is in remembrance of, and with thanksgiving for, all that their Captain, the only

Son of the Supreme Admiral of the Fleet has done for them. The Captain's name is SAVE (S.A.V.E.) which means: 'Son of the Admiral, Victorious over the Enemy'. Long ago He rescued the crew from slavery to the pirate who roams the 'Sea of Life', and signed them up for life as His own crew. The pirate chief, whose flag is 'Death', was defeated at a great battle called the 'Battle of Calvary'. He was mortally wounded, but still roams the 'Sea of Life', seeking to rob and to destroy. But his days are numbered, and one day he and his evil crew, will be sunk without trace.

We are permitted to study the ship's log, and to follow the fascinating history of the whole fleet. The Admiral of the Fleet controls everything from Headquarters. He works very closely with His 'Right Hand Man', His Son, the Captain of the Fleet, who directs all operations from the Main Control Room, and delegates some authority to the ship's officers. The Fleet had started many years ago with only one ship which was launched into the 'Sea of Life' by a very strong wind from a distant port called 'Pentecost'. Its destination was the 'Haven of Eternal Life' beyond the bright shining horizon called 'Hope'. After a while, some of the crew became very alarmed because the ship appeared to be veering wildly off course. They began to protest and question the seamanship of those who were navigating, and had various disputes with the most senior officer.

While the ship was at anchor just outside a port called 'Reformation', the protestors left the ship. They began to build several ships to their own design, and launched them on the 'Sea of Life'. These became known as the 'Protestant Fleet'. They navigate by means of an ocean map called 'The Word of

God', and with the aid of this compass, steer the ship through dangerous waters, avoiding the jagged rocks of 'Heresy', and the soft sandbanks of 'Philosophy'. The sails are called 'Faith', and are kept trimmed to catch each breath of wind, the source of power, which is the 'Holy Spirit'. There are problems for the SS Church of England'. Waves are developing which threaten to grow and overwhelm the ship. They are called 'Euthanasia' and 'Homosexuality' and may cause problems when the chief officers meet aboard the good ship 'Lambeth Conference'. They send an S.O.S. message to the Admiral through the Captain: "Lord, don't you care if we drown?" They don't seem to understand that this message makes the Admiral and the Captain very sad, because they love the officers and crew, and have everything under control. The Captain sends these instructions: "Hoist the sails and spinnakers called 'Faith' and go forward; let them be filled with the wind of the Spirit. There is urgent work to be done. People are drowning in the "Sea of Life'. Send out the life boats called 'Compassion'. Throw out the lifeline called the "Gospel of Salvation". There are many boats without a compass going in the wrong direction or round in circles. Their captain is the pirate chief who is called "A Liar", and the "Father of Lies". Urge these ships to change course and join the ships belonging to the "Admiral of the Fleet", and sign on as crew. There is no signing on fee, and the rewards are everlasting. Have no fear, you will not be lost. Just out of sight beneath the waves is a raft of life called "The Everlasting Arms". This raft will carry you to the place I have reserved for you, and you will see me soon when I come to lead you in triumph into the "Haven of Eternal Life". So I say to the storms without and within you "Peace, be still!" To all the officers and crews "Why are you afraid? Where is your faith?"

The Eternal City
Allegory

This is what the Lord says, the words of Jesus as faithfully recorded by St. Matthew, chapter 7 verses 13,14 "Enter through the narrow gate. For wide is the gate and broad is the road that leads to destruction, and many enter through it. But small is the gate and narrow the road that leads to life, and only a few find it".

You are invited to come, in your imagination, on a mystery journey. Imagine that you are among a group of travellers representing all the nations, tribes, creeds and colours of the world, and that you are travelling towards the Eternal City, the glowing spires and towers of which you can see high up on a hill in the distance. Soon you come to crossroads and facing you, a high brick perimeter wall with a pair of wide, open gates, through which you can see a wide straight road which is called the 'Broad Way', and to the left of it, a noisy funfair called 'Pleasure Park'. To the right of the wide gates and some distance from them, is a single open gate through which you can see a path called the 'Narrow Way', twisting and turning through woodlands, streams and pastures. At the crossroads, the roads to the right and left are both barred and signed 'No Through Road'. The travellers therefore have a choice; the Broad Way or the Narrow Way. Most of them are attracted to the Broad Way and the bright lights and sounds of 'Pleasure Park'; but some choose the Narrow Way which, although dimly lit, appears to be more restful for weary travellers.

At the end of the Broad Way, and up on the hill, is a very high wall surrounding the City, and the wall is called 'The Mystery of Life and Death'. There is no way round it, over it or under it, but there are many doors in it all painted in bright colours, and some with flashing lights. Along the Broad Way, the chief showman of 'Pleasure Park' appears, in the form of a shining angel. His work is to persuade the travellers to spend time in the funfair where they can win all sorts of glittering prizes. The prizes are attractively and colourfully wrapped, but when torn open are found to be rotten and full of corruption; sexual immorality, impurity, idolatry, hatred, jealousy, selfish ambition, envy, drunkenness, and the like. Between the Broad Way and the Narrow Way there is a golden harvest field, through which at intervals, there are pathways. At each pathway stands a harvest worker called an 'Evangelist' warning the travellers to turn from the Broad Way which leads to destruction, and offering the free gift of salvation through faith in Jesus Christ, the Son of God, along the pathways called 'Repentance' which lead to life, health and peace on the Narrow Way. Some stop and listen and are persuaded, but many pretend not to hear, and rush on up the hill towards the wall of the City where the brightly coloured doors await them. These are called 'The Doors of Deception and Delusion', and they are easily pushed open by those who want to go in. But there stands the last Evangelist warning travellers not to go that way. Those who, finally and decisively, ignore all the warning signs, and reject the free gift of salvation, push open the 'Doors of Deception and Delusion'. Once inside, they find a labyrinth of connecting passages with dead ends called 'Disappointment', 'Bitterness', 'Frustration', 'Despair'. In the very centre of the labyrinth there is a walled courtyard at one end of which is a large door made of pure gold inscribed with the Scales of Justice and the Laws of God. Above the door is a sign which reads 'The Supreme Court'. There the people are told to wait until their names are called to appear before the Righteous Judge who sits on the throne in the Judgment Hall.

The travellers on the Narrow Way find the journey difficult but rewarding, and along the way discover the "Key of Faith', which enables them to go on, even when the way is dark and uncertain, and when they come under attack by unseen forces. But along the way they pass through some beautiful orchards where they are offered the 'Fruits of the Spirit' which are called love, joy, peace, patience, kindness, goodness, faithfulness, gentleness, and self control. Eventually they come to the high wall called 'The Mystery of Life and Death', and there, half hidden by some thorn bushes they can see a rough wooden door in the wall. The door has four panels which between them form the shape of a cross. It is damaged and scarred, and stained with blood. It has nails in it, and engraved on it the figure of a sacrificial Lamb, and a text which reads, "I am the Way and the Truth and the Life. No one comes to the Father except through Me". On the lintel above the door there is a sign which says – "Jesus of Nazareth, King of the Jews". The text and the sign can be understood in every language on earth. But the door is locked and can only be opened with the Key of Faith. All who possess this Key can enter through this door, and find to their intense joy that this is none other than the way into the Father's House, where there are many rooms, in which perfect homecoming conditions have been prepared well in advance. In the centre of the Eternal City, a great multitude that no one can number, wearing white robes and holding palm branches, stand in front of the Lamb, and cry out in a loud voice: "Salvation belongs to our God who sits on the throne, and to the Lamb". The City does not need the sun or the moon to shine on it, for the glory of God gives it light, and the Lamb is its lamp. This is the inheritance of the children of God, who have washed their robes, and made them white in the Blood of the Lamb.

Lightning Source UK Ltd.
Milton Keynes UK
UKHW020705080721
386821UK00007B/301